the long weekend

by philip katz

Combating Unemployment During the Inter-War Years

Foreword by Fred Higgs
General Secretary of the International Federation
of Chemical, Energy, Mining and General Workers' Unions

The moral right of the author to be identified as the originator of this work has been asserted under the Copyright, Designs and Patents Act 1988.

Published by Hetherington Press

First pressing May 2001
Design Suzanne Kristel Body
Cover Photo courtesy Hulton Picture Library
Typeset in Joanna 11/13 pt
Printed in the UK by PhilTone Litho

British Library Cataloguing-in-Publication Data
A catalogue record for this book is available from the British Library.

Display as: History; Inter-War Years; Employment; Unemployment;
        Industrial History; Economics; Trade Unions.

Copyright ©Philip Katz
ISBN number 0-9540462-0-X

Any part of this book may be re-produced without the express permission of the author. However, acknowledgement should be given and examples of the published or online published work supplied.

For those wishing to use sections for extensive quoting, development, adding testimonials or bulk reproduction for academic purposes, the book is available in Word text only format - Mac or PC - on CDrom at a cost, including postage of £10 or $15.
Orders can be made at reprints@hetheringtonpress.co.uk

Copies of The Long Weekend can be purchased via orders@hetheringtonpress.co.uk priced £11 or $17.50 including postage and packing.

Those wishing to contact the author may do so at philkatz@hetheringtonpress.co.uk

For Sam, Bella-Rosa, Betty and Sarah.
And for Herbert Marin Cotrini who is with me always.

ACKNOWLEDGEMENTS
Thanks to Ian for his original foresight and investment; to Sharon for her skill and patience; to Rita for her insight; Ros for using her command of English, skills of editing and her determination; and Diana for her support. Finally, to Fred, who found time to put aside a busy global schedule and set his thoughts on employment to paper.

CONTENTS

Acknowledgements

List of tables Page 6

Foreword by Fred Higgs Page 9
General Secretary of the International Federation of Chemical, Energy, Mining and General Workers' Unions.

Introduction – A Tale of Two Closures Page 10
Why, today, is there so little action against unemployment and what could be done about it?

A Problem of Industry? Page 19
Unemployment becomes a word in its own right. Beveridge says that unemployment is less a question of personal and individual motivation, more a collective issue of Industry.

New Features of Unemployment Emerge Page 22
The local becomes national. Sectional becomes general. Short-term unemployment becomes long-term and intractable. Collapse is swift.

The Unemployed Page 28
Who were they? Where did they live? Why were they out of work?

Unemployment, Political Parties and Government Economic Policy Page 44
A problem that will not go away but for which too few will take responsibility. Where will the answer to the questions raised by those out of work come from?

What Did the Unemployed Do About Unemployment? Page 66
If no one else would do it, they would have come up with the answers themselves. But answers on paper are not enough.

The NUWM Early Years and the 1920s Page 79
Breaking the workhouse, building a campaign and an organisation.

Employed and Unemployed Unity Page 89
So near and yet so far. The NUWM and TUC square up to combat unemployment, only to end up squaring up to each other.

From the General Strike to the Great Crash Page 101
Each side rationalises division and defeat. The TUC seeks to develop alternatives to the NUWM. Understanding the motivation of NUWM leaders.

The NUWM in the Hungry Thirties Page 116
Individual representation, cuts in benefits and the threat of war and fascism. The Means Test is destroyed.

Hungry Thirties and the Approach of War Page 146
Unemployment linked to foreign policy. NUWM winds down. Unity between NUWM and TUC remains elusive.

A Restoration Page 162
Seeing the NUWM for what it really was. Seeing the unemployed as they really were.

Afterword Page 175
A point to ponder.

Bibliography Page 176

List of tables

Table 1 Page 23
Unemployed in the staple trades compared with the national average.

Table 2 Page 26
Country shares in world export of manufactures 1899-1950.

Table 3 Page 29
Proportion of insured workers unemployed in the UK 1920-1939.

Table 4 Page 30
Unemployment figures for insured workers.

Table 5 Page 31
Great Britain character of unemployment 1923-1936.

Table 6 Page 32
Number of factories opened, closed and extended in London and Britain between 1932-1937.

Table 7 Page 33
Proportion of unemployment by region (figure taken in July of each year).

Table 8 Page 35
Average annual gains (+) or losses (-) through migration 1923-1936.

Table 9 Page 36
Geographical distribution of unemployment and changes 1921-1938.

Table 10 Page 37
Unemployment of insured workers in staple industries 1920-1938.

Table 11 Page 38
Unemployment in selected industries 1932 and 1937.

Table 12 Page 39
Male unemployment by occupational status, England and Wales in 1931.

Table 13 Page 40
Estimated proportion unemployed in 1927 by age group.

Table 14 Page 41
Average unemployment amongst males and females in Great Britain 1921-1929.

Table 15 Page 46
Indices of UK industrial production 1920-1938 (1909-1913 = 100).

Table 16 Page 50
UK domestic exports 1929-1932.

Table 17 Page 51
UK Government expenditure (central and local) 1910-1935.

Table 18 Page 51
UK Government social expenditure (central and local) 1910-1935.

Table 19 Page 63
Industrial output in Britain 1929-1932 (1929 = 100).

Table 20 Page 65
Distribution of personal wealth, England and Wales 1911-1913 to 1936-1938.

Table 21 Page 91
Trade union membership and rate of unemployment 1920-1939.

Table 22 Page 102
Workers directly and indirectly involved in disputes and the number of days lost 1920-1939.

Table 23 Page 120
Extent of short time working in certain industries in October 1931.

Table 24 Page 121
Economic status of the occupied population of Great Britain in 1931.

Table 25 Page 133
The duration of continuous unemployment at July 1936.

Table 26 Page 136
Unemployment by areas, July 1930.

Table 27 Page 152
Unemployment in large towns, July 1936.

Foreword

This book is a most welcome contribution towards redressing our historical failure to give due recognition to the activities and achievements of the National Unemployed Workers' Movement (NUWM). It also serves as a timely reminder to today's trade unionists that in years to come history will turn to judging our efforts. In this context I believe that Phil's words: "Success or failure for the NUWM was based on its ability to secure change" are particularly succinct.

I also agree with Phil that the obligation on trade unionists to strive for the greater good, necessarily involves them in representing and advancing the interests of communities beyond their own membership, through the political process. In this sense, the trade unionists of the early twentieth century can be judged in terms of their concern and commitment to their fellow unemployed workers. While today's trade union leadership must serve and protect the interests of their membership as well as leading efforts to better the economic and human rights of disadvantaged people right across the globe.

There are endless challenges on our own doorsteps, and beyond. However, if as international trade unionists, we are to become agents for social change on a global level we must learn as much as possible from the successes and failures of our predecessors. But, ultimately, we must certainly look forward rather than backwards. As Phil quite rightly observes it is not our place to fear change, rather, to demand that we are effective players in that process and ensure that change is brought about to the benefit of both organised workers and those excluded from unions through unemployment, economic circumstance or developmental conditions.

Fred Higgs
General Secretary
International Federation of Chemical, Energy, Mine
and General Workers' Unions (ICEM)

Introduction - A Tale Of Two Closures

The genesis for this book begins with the tale of two factory closures. Or, rather, one closure carried out and the other successfully resisted.

In 1998, a decision was taken, at the Head Office of Fujitsu in Marunouchi Street in Tokyo, to close its semi-conductor plant at Newton Aycliffe in Sedgefield in the North East of England.

In the same year, BMW, the German carmaker, took over Rover and soon sought its early closure, thereby threatening to end car manufacture in the west midlands. This would have been devastating for the community, affecting the lives of one hundred thousand manufacturing workers and their families.

The response to the Fujitsu decision was stunned silence. That the factory had been open only two years, was one of the most advanced of its kind and had enjoyed serious financial inducements to open in the first place, counted for little. The only ones who cared were those who worked there and had planned their families and futures around it.

The response to the actions of BMW was quite different. The response to Fujitsu revealed Britain and its trades unions at their worst. Sidelined by external decision makers, they opted, instead, to remain spectators. The Government was nowhere to be seen. At Rover, it was the opposite. Determination by the workforce and leadership by unions prepared to seize the initiative, take responsibility rather than carp and complain, think things through strategically and, where necessary, apply leverage constructively eventually overcame what at one point, seemed an impossible situation. The company decision in favour of closure was reversed. This was evidence of a new kind of 'new unionism'.

How could the response to the two threats of closure be so at odds? Part of the answer obviously lies in the variant character of the companies and their operation, at least on the surface, within two different areas of the economy. Fujitsu were at the cutting edge of technology driving forward the 'new' economy but subject to laws of economics where price collapse seems almost unavoidable. BMW Rover were meanwhile operating in a world auto market saturated by overproduction and excessive prices, threatened all around by competitors enjoying greater productivity operating within the single currency zone.

Yet Fujitsu closed; Rover became Phoenix. If the new plant closed and the old remained open, perhaps the reason for the success at Rover lay beyond the supposedly iron laws of economics. Maybe it reflected the different attitudes of the respective workforces and the strategies adopted by their representatives? Perhaps the 'new' workforce was thinking in the old way and the 'old' workforce in a new way?

This set the author on a path of investigation as to how, historically, organised workers respond to the threat of unemployment. The results of the search were quite revealing and led inevitably to the 1930s. Somewhere, EH Carr says that 'history belongs to the winners'. Perhaps for that reason the story of inter-war unemployment has been done to death, yet the true lives, views and activities of the unemployed of the twenties and thirties remain largely unexplored.

The 'history from below' school has not rescued them even though it developed in the 1970s to again look at major historical trends from the experience of the mass. Worse still, the organisation of the unemployed, the National Unemployed Workers' Movement, national, with an unbroken militancy spanning two decades and combative for most of that time, is almost unknown. With the passing of local legends such as Alf Salisbury and the second retirement of great characters such as Jack Jones, their leaders, both local and national have now gone from the political scene.

In today's trade union movement there are two views of unemployment and how it should be dealt with. The first, though it would also be the first to deny it, looks back to the thirties — a period that for many carries the inspiration of struggle against privation and the hunger marches. It misunderstands the desperation of the men and women who took up that struggle and marched. These people hit the road because they were already 'down the road'. From this quarter, the remedies on offer in the 2000s are often little different from those developed during the emotive two inter-war decades.

Yet the 2000s are so different from the 1930s. The generation of trade unionists whose working experience was rooted in the pre-war period is now gone. Those shaping the labour movement of this century are their grandchildren. The current intake of the TUC Organising Academy may even include their great grandchildren. Their attitude to and experience of unemployment, and the economic remedies they seek to apply, will be generations rather than years apart.

The second approach does not look back at all. It looks forward. It does not fear change; indeed it expects and demands to be a player in that process. It drives technological change. At Rover, only the employers proved to be mindless Luddites. The workforce supported by their unions was prepared to take responsibility gathering together everyone who could make a contribution: councils; communities; academics, and local employers. They first made the case and then put together the bid. Phoenix is a product of their endeavour. They did not wait until they were facing the 'long weekend' before dealing with the unemployment threat, nor were they unique in understanding the process of manufacture in which they were employed much better than those who employed them.

This was certainly the case when, for example, the Swedish employers of Kvaerner Govan Shipyards decided to pull out of shipbuilding in 1999. The unions told them that the yard was viable and that production could remain. In the end Kvaerner conceded the Union case and the concern was passed with minimal job loss to GEC Marconi Marine.

To strengthen this forward looking trend, the author thought it essential to clarify exactly what did happen during the period 1918-39. In this way it would be possible to totally dispense with nostalgia thus clearing a way to tackle the reality of the unemployment problem as it is today.

The 1920s and 30s were an extraordinary period. The unemployed were drawn from the trenches of World War I and from the densely union-organised engineering plants that the war effort threw up. This generation of union militants formed the National Unemployed Workers' Committee Movement (NUWM) – a unique organisation for labour in Britain then and since. A combination of unemployment and membership of the NUWM made militants of many more. Yet all too few today know that the organisation existed and those that do have little idea of what it stood for, what it did and what it achieved. Most people who consider the 1930s and unemployment, think only of Jarrow. How many know that the Labour party conference refused support to the Jarrow marchers?

When looking at the 1930s all is not necessarily what it seems. The truth about many organisations and individuals has become obscured by the dust of succeeding years and the best written out by commentators and historians, their vision clouded by the shabby, lowered standards employed in support of the ideological cold war against communism. Few are aware that the Jarrow march was the smallest of the dozen major regional and national Hunger Marches of the inter-war years, or that, despite their disavowal of militancy, ministers refused to take them seriously.

Yet the NUWM organisation lasted 20 years and, at times, numbered and mobilised hundreds of thousands. That it was national and collective, when so much of the experience of unemployment was local and personal, is an achievement in itself. But though they hailed from the labour movement, for much of its existence NUWM activists expressed their militancy as outsiders. Even on those occasions, especially in the 1920s, prior to the 1926 General Strike, when they were not isolated within the official labour movement itself, they were all too often alienated from those organised workers still in work. And these organised employed workers were the best hope of a return to work for those without it.

The NUWM represented a high point of campaigning effort by those outside work, looking in. Their protests achieved more than even the most enlightened historians have so far conceded. But the limit is obvious. Unemployment is the aftershock of jobs lost. It is vital to save those jobs before the long weekend sets in. Britain needs job creation as much now as it did then. But it will not even begin to tackle the issue unless it can work out how to stem job loss. Economies are always losing and creating jobs. The question is can Britain save the jobs it needs, even when the likes of BMW tell us we do not need to sustain them.

Recreating 'outsiders' campaigns, no matter how heroic, is not what is needed today. With one in five heads of household currently unemployed, many more underemployed and still more doing the work of two or even three, Britain needs a strategy that is focused on the twin aims of job retention and job creation.

Here lies the challenge to Britain's unions and in particular to its Trades Union Congress. At a time of retreat, the TUC developed the concept of 'new unionism', which was aimed at changing the orientation of unions to make them more recruitment conscious. This was successful. However, the context of that new recruitment culture has now changed and next stage new unionism is looking for a focus. The second generation of new unionism will find that focus in the struggle over work: what kind of jobs will exist and can be created? What will be the conditions for those jobs and how will the power of workers be exercised in the workplace?

To the extent that unions take up the challenge of creating jobs they will discover a new and powerful rationale for their existence. Today, no one is secure in employment but unions exist to provide collective security. To keep a job requires skill and application and unions are pivotal in securing opportunities for the acquisition of skills for their members so that they can advance. Even the most superficial analysis of the way the economy is developing with the increased importance attached to knowledge and skill, illustrates how important this new role for unions is. In a number of sectors where employers are not taking adequate responsibility for training: i.e. print; construction; education, unions are stepping in. In fact, they are often stepping back to their origins, when they controlled entry and exit to their respective crafts and defined who was skilled, in order to encourage progress.

There is a bigger picture too. At company level the opportunity exists to influence the nature and condition of employment. At the moment there is the hesitant attempt to define the power of European and other similar works councils. From this searching for a role will come bigger, better things. Unions are uniquely placed to harness and give substance to the quest of workers who want more power and say over their working lives.

This is all well and good at the micro level, but who will deal with changes in employment and unemployment in the context of the economy as a whole? Now, context is everything and unions are as far behind the race for solutions as they were in the 1920s and 1930s. Where, in the post-First World War, workers fought job loss at company level, at national level they were unable to develop alternatives to Snowden, the Treasury and the Gold Standard. Today's Gold Standard is the Single Currency. Unions representing workers who make things in Britain have yet to develop a position that could underpin a National Programme of Job Creation based in and on Britain, despite our unrivalled tradition of manufacture and trade.

If there is a downside to the Rover experience, it is that we should expect many more such episodes. In the same month that Rover was saved, the process of breaking up Ford Dagenham was begun. It was followed in swift succession with an attempt to force through the end of car making in Luton.

In the 1980s, the TUC coined a slogan "Forward to the Eighties – Not Back to the Thirties". But it was not that we did not want to go back – it was that we couldn't. The marches of the Eighties, though well organised and intentioned, had none of the influence of those a half century before. The latter were driven by desperation on the one hand and a determination to redirect government policy on the other. By the 1980s, the marches were a sign of a different type of desperation borne of a vacuum of policy and a lack of job creating alternatives. When the unions said effectively, 'throw more public money at the problem' they were really opening the door to the opposite of what they wanted, allowing Thatcher to say 'you cannot spend what you have not got'. Focus on resources divorced from issues of content and quality will always be a dead-end. Actually even by the 1970s, life had already moved on. With the new economy emerging, the differences between the 1980s and the 1930s were about to be accentuated still further. Recognition of this would have concentrated minds more on quality and strategic investment rather than attempting to shore up the public sector with what were effectively black holes for public money.

Future historians and economists may well debate the effect of this new economy in the same way that the impact of the new industries was debated in the inter-war years. But those looking for a 'new' economy will look in vain. What is revolutionary about the emergent economy is its interrelationship with the existing one. It is often said, in effect, that shipbuilding has given way to chip building. Ironically, there are probably more micro chips in a recently constructed ship than there are in most other movable manufactured products, save that of a satellite.

The dynamism of today's technological change is a product of the material wealth, engineering skill and historically determined pool of intelligence that already exists. Those who rubbish everything belonging to past, including our education system, may well pause to reflect on where the knowledge of those working in our modern industries came from. Those who wish to look for clues as to where Britain is going and the problems she is likely to face on her journey should look at the same factors.

The impact of the new economy is already bigger than that of, say, chemicals in the 1920s. It is more akin to the advent and application of steam power to manufacturing during the industrial revolution and later, the internal combustion engine. And more. Some have likened it to the first harnessing of fire. The question is worth asking. Are we to again repeat the past error of focusing only on the job-loss implications of new forces of production? Or can we seize on the opportunities they create, perhaps wielding them to create more and better jobs, thereby lessening the load currently on offer?

In the 1930s, industries were mothballed, not destroyed. Factories were put on short time and shutdown, not broken up. Mines were not flooded. Some capital was exported, but much remained. Indeed, the experiences of Total War in 1940 swiftly brought those forces back into production. Though a challenged and diminished body relative to the USA, or Germany, Britain was still at the centre of world trade, not subject to the kind of globalising forces experienced today. The global economy of the 1930s was in traded goods. By the 1980s, this had become one of manufactured goods, altogether a qualitatively different challenge to Britain's economy. So where will the jobs come from? In the 1930s, at worst, we were a severely reduced economy still based on wealth-creating manufacture. By the 1980s, to paraphrase Ted Heath, we were in danger of trying to pay our way in the world by taking in other people's washing. Trade barriers erected for the task of maintaining the Empire have come down only to be replaced by those of the European Union, where they are definitely not operated in Britain's favour. Just look at the current constraints facing agriculture, or fishing. Look at the role of the EU in restricting government intervention in defence of Rover. Note too the seriousness of the EU finance ministers admonishing of the Chancellor seeking to block his measures to support investment in infrastructure, the public sector and direct intervention in Rover. Each of these actions runs counter to the Treaty signed at Maastricht and the Growth and Stability pact. Strict controls on the movement and deployment of capital, once a centrepiece of trade unions and national economic policy have been removed altogether. In their place, embarrassed silence and paralysis. 'Intervention', a centre-piece of progressive thinking in the 1930s has become a dirty word.

Things look very different now. The campaigning zeal of the NUWM would not go amiss. But the organisation would have to take into account the weightless, digitalised economy, where science has become industrialised and in turn drives industry. Proportionately fewer work in the wealth producing sector than at any time since the mid-19th century; more work in Indian restaurants than in steel-making. Community life has changed radically. So what jobs are to be saved and which ones need to be created? The unions who represent those in work have to look at old ideas in a fresh way and tackle some newer challenges too.

Where once iron and steel dominated, plastics and micro processors now rule. Science and industry combine to strike at the very centre of the construction of things. Factories, and the machines they contain, are growing ever smaller. Production lines are given their own intelligence and work is structured on higher levels of teamwork and more flexible methods of application. In many manufacturing sectors unskilled work has become mechanised, automated or is done away with altogether. Barriers that once prevented the semi skilled from become craft men and women have disappeared. Networking and the Internet, now freed from the PC, are set to take things further, more quickly and in a direction few labour movement policy makers have yet grasped. Where it was once possible for one person to read all of the books in the world scientists predict that, by 2012, the total stock of human knowledge will be doubling every 73 days. All the time, innovation and skill inputs continue to rise and countries struggle to develop education systems that can cope with the pace and nature of change. Far from de-skilling these developments are putting greater pressure to develop better quality base and higher skills than ever.

Unions are inside this process, seeking to control and direct as representatives of the productive labour that makes such change happen. To the extent that they can achieve this they appear as contributors, as players. To the extent that they remain blind, or even just sceptical, they consign themselves to stagnation and opportunities are missed. Unions may always be with us. But they will only ever be successful in attracting new members if they are effective. As in the 1920s, job loss is more than a natural development of economic change. It is also a reflection of the patterns of ownership and deployment of capital. Workers are the manufacturers, the makers of things. They also reproduce the educated, healthier and more skilled worker required to build Britain's future.

Unions can influence patterns of ownership and the direction of capital. It is not God-given that companies can invest for a moment and decamp at will. A quarter of all the capital in the UK is made up of pension funds to whose Boards workers elect representatives. It matters to us if decisions over the working life of our country are taken in Marunouchi Street in Tokyo or in Birmingham. If there is to be a future for Britain, it is through the making and trading of manufactures. A global economy is not a matter of choice or ideology it is a fact. One could argue over how far globalisation has or is taking place. One could argue over how much power an economy has to create and sustain jobs within this process. What is certain is that, regardless of the conclusion one may draw, Britain cannot just shut up shop. Its population cannot just migrate. So it becomes necessary to consider how a country can find a role for itself in the world economy and provide for its people. For Britain to stand a chance it must concentrate on what it does best. That is why the issue of manufacture, invention, skill and trade are so important. Concentrate on that and some of the anxiety about our future as a nation might just subside. Or at least find some sense of perspective.

The job of the economic historian is to go beyond 'what happened' though it has been necessary to show why unemployment took on the breadth and character it did and how workers chose to organise against it; it may not even be to say what could have happened. What is attempted here is to look at what did happen and show why the NUWM took the direction that it did. Moreover, what can we learn from the path it chose and the way in which it chose to tread that route. What is in it for us in today's rapidly changing world?

The tale of struggle against the blight of unemployment during the inter-war years is that of a real and heroic struggle for dignity. But it is not the way for our children. The heroism of Hunger Marches is made no more glorious because they were not winners. Future generations must work out for themselves, how to take the inside track, if they are to successfully go for the tape.

A Problem Of Industry?

'1914 Popularity and Fags –
1921 Charity and Rags…
1914 Mobilisation and War –
1921 Starvation and Jaw'.

Written on stewards' armbands on 4 October 1921 -
Unemployed march in Whitehall.

Prior to 1914, Government and economists viewed unemployment as a social rather than economic problem and as something that arose from essentially 'abnormal circumstances'. Classical economic theory maintained that the economy would naturally tend towards full employment and that this was the normal state of affairs. This belief rested on the economic doctrine known as Says Law, which suggested that, since production created its own consumption, under-consumption or over-production were impossible. In the words of WT Colyer, an early and popular tutor of the National Council of Labour Colleges, *"Unemployment is often classified, along with famine and pestilence, as a calamity which arises out of the order of nature, from causes which man is hardly beginning to understand and which he can as yet do little to prevent."*

The word 'unemployment' was relatively new to common parlance. It only appeared in the New English Dictionary in 1882, with 'unemployed' following six years later.

After 1880, there was increasing concern about poverty in general and it was recognised that unemployment was a basic cause of poverty.

Attempts were made by successive governments to relieve the inadequacies of the poor law in providing employment and, in 1911; some relief was made through the establishment of a limited National Insurance Scheme. In 1919, these provisions were extended to a larger section of the workforce, covering some 12 million workers in the staple industries. Under the Acts of 1911 and

1920, unemployment benefits were payable for strictly limited periods, based on the number of contributions which the insured worker had previously paid in to the Unemployment Fund.

In 1909, William Beveridge in 'Unemployment: A Problem of Industry' had argued that the problem of unemployment might be cured by an increase in the mobility of labour and advocated a network of labour exchanges to make this easier. The title of the pamphlet itself was a step into unknown territory: the days when unemployment could be ascribed purely to a lack of personal resource, motivation, intelligence or initiative was being left behind. Unemployment was no longer a personal problem but one of industry, of economy.

Beveridge suggested a more direct solution in terms of large-scale counter-cyclical public works. This was strongly urged by the Ministry Report of the Royal Commission on the Poor Laws in 1909, but met with little success. Indeed such thinking was to prove way ahead of its time.

With the end of the First World War, government understanding of the unemployment problem was extremely limited. The high level of unemployment, especially long-term unemployment, which was to be a major permanent problem throughout the two inter-war decades, served to greatly highlight the inadequacies of consecutive governments in dealing with the problem. In the words of Aneurin Bevan, there were those administrations *"who would have preferred to run away"*. All parties, Liberal, Labour and Conservative subscribed to the economic orthodoxies of the Gold Standard and the mantra of a balanced budget. They gave priority to repaying the national debt accumulated during the war. Only the collapse of the second Labour Government under MacDonald, in August 1931, forced Britain away from the Gold Standard and into a limited form of protectionism.

The post-1918 situation of extensive and widespread unemployment was a challenge for the trade union movement whose numbers had risen during the war, from 4,135,000 in 1913 to 8,348,000 by 1920. Funds to help unemployed members emigrate, a feature of craft unionism in all sectors of industry, was no longer adequate to cope with the increased number without work or to allay the fears of their members who had a job. Money allocated by the general unions for the relief of temporarily out of work members soon dried up.

Unemployment reinforced poverty and hunger and led to significant internal migration and the break-up of families. There was a need for urgent solutions, but they were slow to come from a government unconvinced that it could play a role and bereft of ideas as to how to organise any intervention. Successive governments from 1920 through to 1939 sought to cope with twentieth century unemployment using nineteenth century concepts and what remained of the machinery of the Poor Laws. The old theories for the remedy of unemployment, namely *"things will work themselves out"* still dominated the new ones of Marx, Hobson, Keynes and Mosley. Only one section of society formulated coherent policies to challenge unemployment and acted on them, namely the unemployed themselves.

For two decades the National Unemployed Workers' Movement (NUWM) organised opposition to unemployment and sought to offset the worst economic effects and indignities compounded by lack of government action. It initially sought a place within the trade union movement but, in the fallout following the 1926 general strike, was forced to its margins. This meant that it was resigned, albeit effectively, to an agitation role. Only those organised in the unions, in the core industries in which the movement was centred, could block the speed-ups, control forced overtime and oppose shutdown and shakeout. Where, in the early and late 1920s even they were unable to have an impact, the voice of the unemployed was restricted to campaigning against government policy.

This view was well established within the ranks of organised Labour. Arthur Horner, NUWM activist and later leader of the miners wrote, *"I contended that the source of power must be the organised workers because they alone had some organised strength. I said the organised working class in work must be the basis of organisation. I said we must concentrate on strengthening the trade unions and then building an alliance between the employed workers and the unemployed"*. But there was little agreement as to how this unity could be forged or what shape it could take. Where there was dissension over the means, the end became a dismal casualty of an ideological struggle that was to grow throughout the twenties and early thirties.

New Features Of Unemployment Emerge

Unemployment occupies a central place in the history of the inter-war years. George Lansbury, leader of the Labour Party, set the scene when he said in 1922, "*there ought not to be a slum in the land and there ought not to be a hungry person. Yet these things exist all around us.*"

At the end of the 1914-18 war some transitional unemployment was expected as soldiers and war workers were being demobilised and returned to their peacetime occupations. However, the prevailing high level of employment and the 28 days paid leave granted to demobilised soldiers appeared initially to effect a smooth change.

A temporary economic boom, based largely upon accumulated wartime savings and replacement demand, took many who had expected or forecasted gloom – Government included – aback. This was mainly centred on shipbuilding and lasted until April of 1921. Between the armistice and April 1920, 2,900,000 men were added to civilian employment, while the number of females in civilian employment dropped by 500,000. Those in the Forces were reduced by 3,600,000. Throughout the period from armistice until April 1919, unemployment figures never showed more than one million people out of work. This situation was not to last. Indeed, the number unemployed was not to go below one million again before 1940. Unemployment, once grudgingly accepted as a local, seasonal and transitional fact of life, was displaying new, and worrying characteristics.

In the early 1920s, the heaviest concentration of unemployment was to come in those industries that expanded during the war – in shipbuilding, engineering and the metal trades generally. Employment in chemicals had risen by 20 per cent and many in the dockyards, arsenals and government-regulated National Factories were direct government employees. This type of employment had risen between 1914 and 1918. It was, in many ways, a new feature of employment for Britain, where the role of the state in the process of capital accumulation, was much less than that amongst competitors. Although local and municipal government employed many outside the immediate circle of privately owned capital, the number of people employed by central government prior to the war was relatively few. The pressure of home front mobilisation changed all that. The government employed directly and it employed many more indirectly through the allocation of contracts. Few in government expected this situation to continue, but it was, in fact, to become a long-term feature of British capitalism. It brought employment policy and, as the strikes on the Clyde demonstrated, labour relations, into a new more directly politicised dimension.

With the formulation of a Ministry of Munitions in 1915, some 3,000 companies worked to government contracts. By the end of the War, it supervised the work of 20,000 controlled establishments. The government, early on in the war, assumed control of the nation's railways. These industries were geared to production for war and not the exports of peace.

The basic war industries in crisis were soon joined by coal, particularly after 1925, textiles (both cotton and wool) iron and steel and pottery, i.e., those industries best able to compete in an export market which fell far short of expectation.

Table 1 Proportion unemployed in the staple trades compared with the national average

	1921	1929	1932	1936	1938
Coal		18.2	41.2	25.0	22.0
Cotton		14.5	31.1	15.1	27.7
Iron and Steel	36.7	19.9	48.5	29.5	24.8
Shipbuilding	36.1	23.2	59.5	30.6	21.4
Average of all industries		9.9	22.9	12.5	13.3

Source: J Stevenson, British Society 1914-1945 (Penguin 1984)

The collapse was swift and pronounced. In 1921, the tonnage of shipbuilding commenced was only 10 per cent of that in the same quarter of 1920. In January 1921, only 28 per cent of the berths in the United Kingdom were in operation. Of the 56 million spindles in operation, 27.5 million were stopped for the whole six months to July 1921. Where, in 1913, 10.25 million tons of pig iron was produced, by 1921 this fell to only 2.5 million. The monthly average production of pig iron in 1920 was 669,500 tons; by 1921 this had fallen to 217,600 tons. Where 300 blast furnaces were in operation in

October 1920, only 82 were working in October 1921. Matters would have been worse had the peacetime army not retained 50,000 more than its pre-war figure, and this as late as 1921.

When, towards the end of the decade, the House of Commons debated unemployment, Baldwin said that "*Most people, certainly one government after another, thought... that it would merely be by the process of time — some estimating it as a very long time, and some as a very short time — before business would return to normal*". The view then shared by many in government circles was that unemployment was due to the general upset of credit and of the interruption of trade channels between countries. All that was needed was the re-establishment of the gold standard so that the value of the pound could be restored to its pre-war level. Yet the British economy was a diminished force. Many, even in the highest business circles, did not share the view that the interruption to Britain's trade was temporary. They knew she was already falling behind and that other factors had to be taken into account.

For example, the availability of capital for investment was not in question, even in 1921. When, in that year the Anglo-Persian Oil Company made a request for £4 million to cover its capital investment, £63 million was offered by interested parties. So what was happening? Many industrialists, fearing the slump of 1921, finding difficulty in exporting and selling their goods at a profit, would simply not consider long-term investment. Of the capital available for investment, a small percentage only was trusted to industry. Possible 'investment and modernisation' of industry became, by the mid-1920s, 'little investment and rationalisation'. At the same time, employers sought to survive through gains in productivity. Where they were unable to do this by bringing new techniques of management, production and improvements to plant or machinery into play, they simply shed jobs. Or, as in the case of Anglo-Persian Oil, they directed their capital abroad.

The millions of houses, and the hospitals, schools and new industries that the people expected would be built after 1918, were forgotten. Aldcroft writes in 'The Inter-War Economy', "*Not all the unemployment can be attributed simply to the contraction in output of the old staples... a substantial increase in output was secured through a rise in productivity rather than through increased labour inputs*". In some cases, factories were simply prevented from working.

In those sections of industry that did increase productivity, profitability was maintained at the expense of labour. Company survival and unemployment are not necessarily incompatible and productivity did not necessarily mean investing in new machinery or adapting to new production techniques. It could simply mean jobs lost. With the uncertainties of the early twenties, sandwiched between a lack of government leadership and static markets, this became the first option for many employers.

Others with capital to invest hid behind the Government that, itself, was ill disposed to action. Of the total amount of capital applications estimated at £405 million in 1921, 70 per cent went into government securities, five to 6 per cent went to corporation stocks and 10 per cent to 'commercial' issues; only 1.6 per cent went to iron, coal, steel and engineering and 2 per cent went to shipbuilding. Of the total capital available, only one-ninth was devoted to direct industrial production. All of these tendencies ensured that unemployment became a deep fault line throughout the inter-war years.

Despite the repeal of the excess profits duty on companies in the budget of 1921, the tendency to contract and practise economy in the face of an uncertain economic climate meant that the economy was never really stabilised between 1918 and 1939. Such practices actually exacerbated the instability in most basic industries such as construction and textiles and held back modernisation of plant and machinery. It retarded the rate of development in new industries, such as electrical and motor engineering, affecting future world competitiveness with the United States and Germany. Effectively, throughout the twenties and early thirties, these trends prevented the 'new' industries absorbing the unemployed workers inherited from the old.

We can see examples of short-term planning throughout all of industry in this period. Notable and much-needed mergers occurred: ICI was formed in 1926; GEC in electricity; and Unilever in 1925. General Motors took over Vauxhall in 1925. But none of these could compensate for the combination of government mismanagement and the failure to invest in new plant, technology, research and investment throughout the primary, secondary and tertiary sectors.

In overexposed export sectors like coal, new ways of working were slow to be introduced. Imports of Polish coal grew, yet by the general strike in 1926, 75 per cent of all coal was still being cut by hand. The failure of the coal industry was supposedly that its exports could not compete abroad and yet calls were made for Germany to pay part of her war reparations in coal. The German market was deliberately held back, making it more difficult for British exports. In 1921, Russia stood in urgent need of agricultural machinery, but although 73,000 tons of agricultural machinery was exported to Russia in 1913, only 50,000 tons was exported in 1921.

In that year, India imported 60,276 tons of textile machinery from Britain as against 17,945 tons the previous year. She was the only textile producing country in the world whose industry was working fully throughout 1921, whilst production in Britain dropped as much as 50 per cent. In search of short-term profit, British industrialists were equipping their future rivals, who would soon out-distance them, or for political reasons were refusing to trade in the markets that were available. This was mirrored in the setting up of mining interests in Latin America, particularly in Chile and Argentina. Ironically, Britain came to dominate these external local markets at the same time as she was shedding her own.

The large-scale loss of shipping during the war was to be offset by a huge shipbuilding programme, begun in 1918. But with exports drying up it was doubtful where they were to ship. And with domestic export production about to go through the floor, what were they to carry?

The truth is that Britain lost her share of trade in sectors even where world trade was growing as well as those in decline. The government had no answers because it did not accept its share of responsibility for the performance of industry.

For some, the failure to export was the principal cause of the growth of unemployment. Others accuse British industrialists in the export trades of 'crying wolf'. Either way, exporting capital abroad was bound to compound the issue.

Table 2 Country shares in world exports of manufactures 1899-1950

	1899	**1913**	**1929**	**1937**	**1950**
UK	32.5	29.9	23.6	22.4	25.0
USA	11.2	12.6	20.7	19.6	29.1
Germany	22.2	26.4	21.0	22.4	7.1
France	15.8	12.9	11.2	6.4	10.2
Belgium	5.6	4.9	5.5	5.9	5.8
Italy	3.7	3.6	3.7	3.6	3.8
Japan	1.5	2.4	3.9	7.2	3.3

Source: H Tyszinski 'World Trade in Manufactured Commodities; 1899-1950'. Tyszinski's figures are based on the exports of all countries and therefore covers only 80-85 per cent of total world trade.

The contraction of profits in the old industries and the migration of capital to new industries and abroad led to massive unemployment. Blaming unemployment on a failure to export alone can only be a partial answer, especially when we consider that after two decades, the changes necessary to create employment in industry that could have been made remained outstanding. Aldcroft wrote *"the disastrous experience of the British shipbuilding industry cannot... be attributed solely to the collapse of export markets; more important in absolute terms was the stagnation in the home market"*.

The Unemployed

General unemployment percentages disguise the varying levels of unemployment between industries, regions, trades, ages, sexes and it is to these we now turn. The figures will give us an overview of the impact of unemployment on society. To comprehend why the unemployed responded to their circumstances in the way they did, we must go beyond the statistics to look at the specific causes and differential impact in sectors of industry and of regions.

Priestley, in his book 'English Journey', written in the autumn of 1933, discovered four Englands. The first was the old England of the Southern Counties and the guidebooks. The second was nineteenth century England, the industrial North, the country of coal tips and silent blast furnaces and thousands of rows of little houses all alike. The third, twentieth century England was the England of the bustling Home Counties, of bypasses and housing estates and suburban villas and cocktail bars gleaming with chromium trim. The fourth was the England of the dole. To this England we can add all of industrial Scotland, all of South Wales and parts of North Wales as well. Despite the concentration of unemployment in these areas, nearly all workers were fearful of, and often but one step away from the dole. For this generation, there were no redundancy payments. Low wages and inconsistent employment meant that compared with today, savings were very low. As benefits were also low, pressure was on employers to drive wages as low as possible. Many who did not work, existed little above the poverty line. These people appeared voiceless.

According to statistics based on National Insurance payments, at least 10 per cent of the insured work force was unemployed in any year between 1921 and 1939. See Table 3. This figure excludes the many agricultural workers, housewives and others who either came under different schemes or none at all. During these years, the average level of unemployment was over 14 per cent of the insured workforce. The peak levels of unemployment came in April, May and June of 1921 when it exceeded 20 per cent. An inter-war minimum of approximately 10 per cent of all insured workers was reached in 1924, 1927 and 1937.

Table 3 UK – Proportion of insured workers unemployed; 1920-1939

Year	%	Year	%	Year	%
1920	3.6	1928	10.8	1936	13.1
1921	16.9	1929	10.4	1937	10.8
1922	14.3	1930	16.1	1938	12.9
1923	11.7	1931	21.3	1939	10.5
1924	10.3	1932	22.1		
1925	11.3	1933	19.9		
1926	12.8	1934	16.7		
1927	9.7	1935	15.5		

Source: British Labour Statistics Historical Abstract 1886-1968 (1971)

Table 3 refers only to those workers out of work who were part of the National Insurance Scheme and therefore provides an incomplete picture. Before the introduction of the Unemployment Insurance Scheme, statistical information was only available on the basis of returns from a limited number of trade unions that paid unemployment benefits to their members. Under the National Insurance Act of 1920, the Insurance Scheme was extended to cover nearly 12 million workers out of an economically active population of 19 million – thus the Scheme and the statistics derived cover only 60 per cent of the workforce.

In addition, Ministry of Labour data for the inter-war period does not include unemployed workers who failed to register at employment exchanges. It does not count those on short-time working. Nor does it include married women who gained no benefit from signing on but would relish the opportunity to work. Most analysts of these figures agree that they underestimate the number actually out of work by between 12 and 14 per cent. The recent debate concerning the quantification of unemployment is, therefore, not a new one. Behind the percentages and figures lay misery for millions.

Table 4 Unemployment total for insured workers

Date	Total	Date	Total
December 1920	691,000	December 1929	1,334,000
March 1921	1,355,000	December 1930	2,500,000
June 1921	2,171,000	December 1931	2,500,000
December 1921	2,038,000	January 1932	2,850,000
December 1922	1,464,000	January 1933	2,950,000
December 1923	1,229,000	January 1934	2,400,000
December 1924	1,263,000	January 1935	2,290,000
December 1925	1,243,000	January 1936	2,130,000
December 1926	1,432,000	January 1937	1,670,000
December 1927	1,194,000	January 1938	1,810,000

Source: C L Mowat – Britain Between the Wars 1918-1940 (Methuen 1968)

One of the principal features of unemployment in the inter-war years is the high percentage of workers who were unemployed for extended periods and the consequent effect this had when concentrated regionally or in a single industry such as coal mining or shipbuilding.

Mortimer, in his history of the Boilermakers' Society, estimates that, at times in the Twenties, fully 60 per cent of members were drawing union unemployment benefits.

In September 1929, AJ Cook, Secretary of the Miners' Federation of Great Britain, stated when giving evidence to the Committee on Unemployment Insurance that, *"since 1926, 1,068 mines have been closed down, 553 abandoned"*, and claimed that *"A most serious feature of unemployment in the coalmining industry is its long duration; large numbers of miners have been unemployed for years"*.

Unemployment fell generally into three categories. The first was made up of those who were out of work for a few weeks or months at a time or who were drawing partial unemployment relief. The second group were the young who had never had work, or who had worked as youths only until they qualified for a man's wage. The third were the long-term unemployed who had been out of work for a year or longer and were unlikely ever to find work again. Many of them could not return to normal working life until after World War II had begun. Others were to go straight into the armed services and did not work again until after 1945.

Table 5 Great Britain character of unemployment; 1923-1936

	Rate of Unemployment	Average Period of Unemployment (days)	Proportion of Year Out of Work	Proportion of Labour Force Out of Work Within a Year
1923-26	11.3	84.0	26.9	42.0
1928	10.7	84.3	27.0	39.6
1929	10.3	84.9	27.2	37.9
1930	15.8	99.2	31.8	49.7
1931	21.1	126.0	40.4	52.2
1932	21.9	129.8	41.6	52.6
1933	19.8	131.4	42.1	47.0
1934	16.6	117.9	37.8	43.9
1935	15.3	117.0	37.5	40.8
1936	12.9	111.1	35.6	36.2

Sources: M Thomas, 'Labour Market Structure and the Nature of Unemployment in Inter-War Britain', in B Eichengreen and T J Hatton (eds), Inter-war Unemployment in International Perspective (1988), p.106

Throughout the 1920s, the problem of long-term unemployment was fermenting. It was given a decisive push by the collapse of certain engineering markets prior to the 1926 general strike, and in coal mining thereafter. By the economic slump, resulting from the world crisis and the Wall Street crash, it had become a deeper and more generalised problem. But whereas engineers could at least move to where the work was, coal miners, ship builders and cotton workers were to have few such opportunities. Some miners did head south to the anthracite-rich coal seams of Kent. As a result of this migration, the Kent coal mining community contained every accent to be found in the British Isles. For most, the only option was to change occupation or move, either within the country, or abroad. Yet often age made such options impossible.

There were 300,000 long-term unemployed in Britain in January 1932 and 480,000 in July 1933. They were 24 per cent of those receiving unemployment pay in July 1936. Their numbers were greatest amongst men aged 60-64 – relief ceased at 65 – and diminished in each lower age group. They were most numerous among miners, shipbuilders, cotton trade operatives and, therefore, in the areas of greatest distress.

According to a report made to the Pilgrim Trust in 1938 entitled 'Men Without Work', 57 out of 1,000 workers in 1936 were long-term unemployed in North East England, 123 out of 1,000 in Wales, 281 in Rhondda where they numbered 11,000. Amongst these long-term unemployed, 52,900 had been out of work for over five years in 1936, 205,000 for two years or longer in 1936, and 305,000 had been out for 12 months or more. In the same year in Crook, 71 per cent of the unemployed had been unemployed for more than five years; in the Rhondda the figure was 45 per cent.

In Glasgow, Hutt has estimated that 50 per cent of the working population were unemployed in 1931. In Durham and Tyneside in 1936, of 165,873 unemployed, 63,046 had been unemployed for two years, 40,729 for more than three years, 18,540 for four and 9,246 for more than five years. It is difficult to portray the hardship that such figures represented. These people were not dipping in and out of the labour market doing odd jobs and a day here or there. They were often scavenging to survive in towns almost wholly on the dole. Their condition was acquiring the hallmarks of permanent exclusion.

Taking an average of the eight years 1929-36 unemployment in London and the South East was roughly half the national level, while in the North and Wales it was double that of the South.

The number of factories opened, extended or closed can give us some idea of the regional disparity that existed.

Table 6 Number of factories opened, closed and extended in London and Britain 1932-1937

	LONDON	BRITAIN
Factories opened	1,400	3,220
Factories closed	868	2,576
Factories extended	307	1,057
Net increase in number of factories	532	644

Source: From Report of the Royal Commission on the Distribution of the Population (1940), page 166

Of the net increase of 644 factories employing 25 persons or more in the years 1932-7, no less than 532 were located in the Greater London region. These provided employment for 97,700 workers, equivalent to two fifths of all employment provided by new factories opened in Great Britain. In addition, nearly one third of the extensions to existing factories were located in this region. By contrast, Wales, Scotland and parts of Northern England suffered a net loss of factories; the number closed exceeding the number opened throughout this period.

Any regional analysis will, of course, conceal important local characteristics some of which can almost disprove regional trends. For example, in the South East burgeoning with a house-building boom we also find a decline in footwear manufacture. Yet real differences in regional unemployment did exist.

Table 7 Unemployment per centage by region (Figure taken in July of each year)

REGION	1912-1913	1929	1932	1936	Average 1929-1936
London	8.7	4.7	13.1	6.5	8.8
South East	4.7	3.8	13.1	5.6	7.8
South West	4.6	6.8	16.4	7.8	11.1
Midlands	3.1	9.5	21.6	9.4	15.2
North East	2.5	12.6	30.6	16.6	22.7
North West	2.7	12.7	26.3	16.2	21.6
Scotland	1.8	11.2	29.0	18.0	21.8
Wales	3.1	18.8	38.1	28.5	30.1
Great Britain as a whole	3.9	9.7	22.9	12.6	16.9

Source: W H Beveridge, Full Employment in a Free Society (1944), page 73

Both in prosperous and depressed regions there were areas and towns that did not conform to regional trends. For example, the South East and South West of England contained counties with high unemployment such as Norfolk, Suffolk, Cornwall, Devon and Gloucester. In areas such as Perthshire in the North, the unemployment level was well below the average for the region.

Variations in unemployment levels between towns in the same region were often very large. Wigan had an unemployment rate of nearly 23 per cent in 1929, whereas in Rochdale, it was only 8.3 per cent. In the South West in 1937, Redruth had an unemployment rate of 29 per cent, compared to 5.4 per cent in Bath. In the North East, the range was from 24.3 per cent in Barnsley to 6 per cent in Halifax. In South Wales, from 16 per cent in Llanelly to 41.6 per cent in Merthyr Tydfil.

These cases are not the most pronounced. For example, in 1937, Chelmsford in Essex had a rate of 1.6 per cent as opposed to 36.4 per cent in

Pitsea. Stafford and Kidgrove in Staffordshire had rates of 3.4 per cent and 44.5 per cent respectively. In Glamorgan, Resolven had a rate of 4.5 per cent, whereas Ferndale, no great distance away, had 48.1 per cent.

These fluctuations have their basis in the particular characteristics of the industrial structure of the localities or towns concerned. Levels of rural employment were influential in shaping the degree of seasonal and long-term unemployment in a number of regions. Heavy industry affected others. The intensity in Redruth, for example, was due largely to its dependence on the tin and heavy engineering industries, whereas Bath had a relatively diversified economic structure with a wide range of consumer goods production and service industries. Similarly, Barnsley's dependence on coal and heavy engineering gave rise to much persistent unemployment, while Halifax drew its strength from the growing machine tool trade.

Very often the wealth of a town was determined by the fortune of a single industry or even a single employer. Unemployment throughout the 1930s was exacerbated by these degrees of dependence (many of which existed as a result of historically determined structures and cultures). The North had many resources tied up in the basic industries that were in rapid decline, whereas in London, industry was far more diversified and many were employed in non-manufacturing sectors. Indeed, the shape of decline in the North mirrored a decline experienced by London in the late nineteenth century. As the capital city and seat of government, London had a concentration of personal and industrial wealth and had a greater spread of industries and occupation to rely on when times were hard. In 1934, it was estimated that 47.2 per cent of insured workers in London - 10 per cent higher than the national average - fell into the service and trade categories, working in occupations as diverse as bus driving and entertainment. This diversity allowed London to buck national employment trends and even maintain a level of growth twice the national average throughout the 1920s and 1930s. Conversely a greater reliance on a single industry, trade or employer, resulted in a greater risk of job loss.

Another factor of regional influence on unemployment is population migration. During the inter-war years, there were two distinct geographical shifts in population, both of which reversed the dominant trends of the nineteenth century. Firstly, there was a shift away from town centres to the suburbs. More importantly, there was a marked migration from the North into the South generally and London in particular. See Table 8.

Table 8 Average annual gains (+) or losses (-) through migration 1923-1936

	1923-1933	1931-1936
London and Home Counties	+ 62,205	+ 71,623
South East	+ 8,733	+ 18,334
South West	+ 10,582	+ 11,445
Midlands	- 4,964	+ 5,521
North West	- 19,275	- 6,942
North East	- 30,516	- 24,180
Scotland	- 37,559	+ 1,299
Wales	- 31,350	- 22,092
Net inward (+) outward (-) balance of overseas migration	- 42,144	+55,008

Between 1921 and 1937, the population in Outer London grew by 1.4 million while the numbers in Central London fell by 400,000. This can be explained by the growth of industry on the 'stretching boundaries' of London and the cheaper transport and accommodation that, in turn, prompted and reinforced the trend. The 'polo' effect often commentated on by today's sociologists was, in fact, well in place seventy years ago.

The reasons for inter-regional migration were largely the absence of jobs, with the result that the depressed areas lost the biggest numbers, particularly amongst the young. Between 1923 and 1936 London, the South East and South West gained over 1.1 million migrants. Wales, Scotland and North East England lost 1.2 million. Between 1921 and 1939 Wales saw 450,000, mainly of its sons, go south and east.

Differing levels of regional unemployment had a material basis, often found in the susceptibility of the principal local trades to the decline of the national staple industries. Regional differences also had a further material impact, in that its direct product was migration to those areas with diversified and 'new' industries. See Table 9.

Table 9 Geographical distribution of unemployment and changes; 1921-1938

REGIONS	POPULATION IN 1938 (millions)	CHANGE 1921-1938 (per cent)
South East	14.9	+ 18.1
Midlands	7.21	+11.6
West Riding	3.46	+ 6.0
E Counties (R)	1.85	+ 3.7
Lancashire & Cheshire	6.16	+ 3.5
South West	2.08	+ 3.3
Northern Rural Counties	1.29	+ 3.1
Scotland	4.99	+ 2.1
Northumberland & Durham	2.20	- 1.0
Central Wales	0.68	- 4.8
South Wales	1.78	- 8.1

Source: C L Mowat Britain Between the Wars; 1918-1940 (Methuen 1968)

In retrospect, inter-regional migration was less than might have been anticipated. There are several reasons for this in terms of both weak 'push' and 'pull' factors. Wage differentials were not sufficient to attract large numbers of employed workers into expanding areas. Those who did consider moving from depressed to expanding areas had to face economic costs arising from loss of earnings. In addition to higher transport costs and a need to rent accommodation in a more expensive area, there was also the consideration of family dislocation. For some, there was a possibility of loss of status. For example, a miner who moved to the London area was likely to find employment only as an unskilled labourer. Above all, the fact remained that unemployment was high even in the expanding areas, so migration did not automatically offer permanent employment and was often considered too high a price to pay for a broken home and no family life.

In the early 1920s, the heaviest unemployment rates were recorded in the industries that had expanded during the war, namely shipbuilding, engineering and the metal trades. After 1925, coal and cotton came to the fore. By the end of the 1920s it was the staple export trades from coal mining to the woollen trade that were experiencing depression. The staple trades were the basis of Britain's industrial development in the nineteenth century, reaching a peak in the years leading up to the First World War. Coal mining, cotton, wool, tinplate, iron, steel and pottery were all heavily dependent on the export market, in some cases exceptionally so. In 1907, 80 per cent of the cotton industry's output went abroad, together with 57 per cent of woollen and worsted production, 31 per cent of coal and 40 per cent of iron and steel, shipbuilding and engineering.

Geographically these industries were strongly concentrated in the northern regions of the country. For example, in terms of employment, over 80 per cent of the cotton industry was located in Lancashire, 80 per cent of the woollen industry in Yorkshire and 50 per cent of shipbuilding in Northumberland, Durham and on the Clyde. In the case of coal, 19 per cent of employment was in Durham and 20 per cent in South Wales, with a further 28 per cent spread throughout Yorkshire, Lancashire and Nottinghamshire. See tables 10 and 11.

Table 10 Unemployment of insured workers in staple industries; 1920-1938

	1924	1929	1932	1938
Coal	6.8	18.2	41.2	22.0
Cotton	15.8	14.5	31.1	27.7
Wool & Worsted	7.0	15.6	26.6	21.4
Shipbuilding	26.4	23.2	59.5	24.4
Iron & Steel	19.7	19.9	48.5	24.8
Average per cent across all industries	9.9	9.9	22.9	13.3

Source: Chapman & Knight, Wages and Salaries in the UK 1900-1938 (1953)

Table 11 Unemployment in selected industries

	1932	1937
Building	29.0	13.8
Motor Vehicles	20.0	4.8
Electrical Engineering	16.3	3.1
Food Industry	16.6	12.4
Hotel, etc., Service	17.3	14.2
Distributive Trades	12.2	8.8
Coal Mining	33.9	14.7
Wool & Worsted	20.2	10.2
Cotton	28.5	11.5
Shipbuilding	62.2	23.8
Jute	42.2	26.8
Pig Iron Making	43.5	9.8

Source: W H Beveridge, *Full Employment in a Free Society (1944)*, table 33

According to calculations based on the census of 1931, there were 30.5 per cent of unskilled labourers unemployed, 14.4 per cent of skilled and semi-skilled industrial workers, 5.8 per cent amongst white collar workers and 0.5-2 per cent of proprietors of businesses, shops and farmers. See Table 12.

The greatest density of unemployment was locked into those industries where exports were most seriously challenged. Peter Kingsford, in his detailed study of the Hunger Marches 1920-1940, gives us a breakdown of the occupations of those marching. In the first national march in October 1922, the following trades were represented: boilermakers; fitters; blacksmiths; turners; engineers and labourers; dockyard workers; and coalminers. They, together, make up a kind of animated tableau of the industries most affected by the economic depression. They were nearly all ex-servicemen. The tragedy is that, almost all of these were members of the same trades represented on the last national march in 1936. Not a lot had changed. More and more as the hunger marches grew, communities invested in their marching sons and daughters, as a kind of collective advertising of their travail.

Table 12 Male unemployment by occupational status, England and Wales in 1931

Proportion of unemployed males to total occupied males	per cent
Unskilled manual workers	30.5
Skilled and semi-skilled manual workers	14.4
Personal service workers, barbers, waiters, etc.	9.9
Salesmen and shop assistants	7.9
Agricultural workers	7.6
Clerks and typists	5.5
Higher office workers	5.1
Professionals	5.5
Retail traders, innkeepers, bookmakers, etc.	2.3
Farmers	0.5
Proprietors and managers of other businesses	1.3

Source: C Clark, *National Income and Outlay* (Macmillan 1937)

Note: 'Of the unemployment among professional men, 11,500 are accounted for by actors and musicians, put out of work by cinemas and in other professions the percentage rate of recorded unemployment Is only a little over 2 per cent' (original note by Colin Clark).

Age had an obvious effect on the ability to get a job, especially where work was less mechanised and required greater degrees of strength and fitness. A 1927 survey by the Ministry of Labour showed that there was a low rate of unemployment amongst the very young with the rate gradually increasing, especially for men above the age of 45. See Table 13. The percentage dropped to a low level, only above the age of 70. To those above the age of 45 the dole would become the only means of support. With failing health and little chance of learning new skills, it is not surprising that so many became resigned to unemployment for the rest of their lives. Yet, in better times, they would have been capable of working for many years more to support their families. See Table 13.

Table 13 Estimated per cent unemployed in 1927 by age group

AGES	per cent MALE	per cent FEMALE
16-17	2.2	2.1
18-19	7.6	5.3
20-24	9.3	5.1
25-29	11.0	4.3
30-34	9.3	4.1
35-39	9.2	4.5
40-46	9.5	4.3
47-49	10.8	4.6
50-54	11.3	5.2
55-59	13.0	4.8
60-64	15.1	5.5
65-69	17.4	5.9
70 and over	2.2	-
All ages	9.8	4.4

Source: Ministry of Labour Survey; 4th April 1927

The Ministry of Labour Survey established that those aged 50 and above had, by far, the highest share of periods of long-term unemployment. Juveniles were often taken on for two reasons. Firstly, they were paid lower wages. Secondly, some trade unions were able to force employers to provide apprenticeships as a way of guaranteeing maintenance of skills and high standards of workmanship. They also sought to maintain an availability of jobs for future generations, many of whom, particularly in trades such as coalmining, papermaking, printing, engineering and shipbuilding, followed their parents into the same trade. It is a wonder that this system of skill transference between generations, which had taken centuries to fashion and had, for so long, been a source of strength for Britain's industry, survived the inter-war years relatively unscathed, especially when one considers that the apprenticeship system became one of the first casualties of economic slump in the 1980s.

For 50 year olds, the figures substantiate the claim that unemployment repeats itself and that the longer one is out of work, the more difficult it is to find a job. The percentage of the female workforce unemployed remained constant throughout the twenties and thirties. This proves that only a small percentage of females worked in the declining staple industries. Women were concentrated primarily in the cotton and wool trades. In domestic services and light industry, work was repetitive and needed little training and less skill. As we have seen, these industries did not suffer as much as the staple industries with regard to unemployment. Although both the cotton and wool industries had their moments of trauma, the rise in levels of unemployment did not affect the overall level of female unemployment in the way that the fortunes of the coal industry affected the figures for men.

Statistically, in the whole period of the 1920s and early 1930s, (except for 1921 with the breaking up of the war industries when women were forced out of factories and back into civilian life), the number of females unemployed as a proportion of the total female workforce was always significantly less than the proportion of unemployed men in the male labour force.

Table 14 Average unemployment amongst males and females in Great Britain 1921-1929

	per cent MALES	per cent FEMALES
1921	16.8	15.9
1922	16.2	8.7
1923	12.4	9.0
1924	11.2	8.5
1925	12.0	8.1
1926	13.2	9.5
1927	10.9	6.2
1928	12.2	7.2
1929	11.5	7.2

A greater number of women were in age groups that could more easily maintain themselves in work. There was a smaller percentage of the female population in the older age groups. The female population between 1921 and 1931 rose by 9.7 per cent opposed to a rise of 11.2 per cent for males; therefore there were 228,000 less females over the working age of 14 than if the male and female rate of population growth had been the same.

In total, the number of workingmen throughout the 1920s, was 2.5 times the size of the female working population. Much of the data available around this issue is inaccurate as, for example, industries such as agriculture, with a high percentage of female workers, did not come under the insurance scheme and, therefore, periods of unemployment went undocumented.

Unemployment during the inter-war years has long focussed on men. This has certainly distorted any attempt to create an accurate picture of the effects of unemployment on single and married females, the family and significant industrial sectors. For example, the Lancashire cotton districts were important centres of female employment – a sector with a long history dating back to the 1770s. Cotton was Britain's largest manufacturing enterprise and at the outbreak of war, accounted for 40 per cent of world textile production. Whole towns, such as Oldham, were dependent on spinning and weaving. The sector was based on a tight-knit multitude of small family-based companies, slow to change technology and embrace innovation. The First World War had cut out key sectors of export at a time when it is estimated that cotton accounted for a quarter of all UK exports. Over a quarter of a million women were employed in cotton manufacture. Employers, throughout the 1920s, sought to avoid closure by forcing drastic wage cuts and increasing the rate of exploitation by a 'more loom' system. By the early 1930s, unemployment rates in towns such as Burnley could reach 50 per cent and where women played as important a role in an industry as, say, men did in coal, and their gender was no analgesic. Unsurprisingly, the unemployed workers' movement in this area was organised and led by women.

In 1933, the birth rate, which had been steadily declining, reached its lowest point in any peacetime year. The year of highest unemployment was also the year of fewest babies. The connection between the two appears to be reinforced in the following year as depression lifted and the birth rate shifted upwards. However, the once commonly assumed relationship of birth rate to depression is not a simple mechanical 'cause and effect'. For example, the trend towards smaller families was far more apparent in the relatively prosperous South of England than in the areas of heaviest unemployment in the North or Wales. True, all social classes were having fewer children but this tendency was most marked among those least directly affected by unemployment.

These then, were the unemployed. For twenty years they were everywhere one cared to look, in every corner of the nation no matter how dark. They existed in such numbers that they would be ignored at a cost. They could no longer be called the work-shy, to be palmed off on the Guardians. Although existing everywhere, unemployment was not a local problem. Aggregating local and sectional unemployment gave one the unemployed, a national phenomenon of such import that the issue alone made and broke governments in 1924 and again in 1931. If unemployment could no longer be excused as seasonal, temporary or incidental, how would politicians deal with it? What strategies were available to political parties and government? What hope was available to that most desperate group, the unemployed themselves?

STOP THIS STARVATION OF MOTHER and CHILD

By MAUD BROWN
(Women's Dept, N.U.W.M.)
PRICE ONE PENNY
Published by the National Unemployed Workers' Movement,
11a, White Lion Street, London, E.1.

Unemployment, Political Parties And Government Economic Policy

> "... There was never at any time a singular, all transcending, determination to deal with unemployment as such ... unemployment was seen by most contemporaries as a symptom rather than a disease...".

At the beginning of the inter-war period, government understanding of its role in relation to unemployment was extremely limited and largely erroneous. While it was grudgingly accepted that the government should attempt to alleviate suffering by establishing labour exchanges and through contributory insurance, prevailing economic theory suggested that a real solution could only come from market flexibility and not from government action.

By the end of the 1920s, the official attitude had hardened into what became known as the 'Treasury View'. According to this view, substantial reductions in unemployment could only come as a result of wage flexibility. Direct government intervention in the form of investment in public works schemes was rejected. The explanation for this was that, since there only existed a fixed amount of savings available for investment in the economy, public works investment would simply divert capital from 'normal' or private channels without increasing the aggregate level of investment and employment. From this point of view, the scope for independent action by the government was very limited. Any drastic action was likely to damage the long-term prospects for British industry. This rationalisation of inactivity dominated Government thinking in relation to unemployment throughout the entire inter-war period.

Government policy would have to take into account both the scale of unemployment in the worst years and the different types of unemployment that existed throughout the inter-war decades.

Large sections of the workforce were employed seasonally or on a casual basis, especially in the important areas of agriculture and docks. Some unemployment was easy to predict because of the restrictions that the World

War had brought to trade. When Britain emerged from the war, she was no longer world leader and had lost as much as 20 per cent of her markets. Pre-war levels of trade were not regained until 1925.

The unemployment visited on the staple industries was partly associated with the trade cycle and was inevitable in the wake of war. Industry had been greatly boosted during the war and any narrowing of markets was bound to have an effect. There was, in addition, the legacy of the growth in national debt forced by the need to finance the war effort. But the real problem was structural. There were groups of skills, such as those of the Nottinghamshire lace makers that had been superseded and were disappearing altogether. In other sectors, 'one company' and 'single industry' towns were particularly susceptible. Ellen Wilkinson powerfully captured the effect of this kind of unemployment on 'company towns' such as Jarrow, felled by the closure of its shipbuilding industry, in her book, 'The Town that was Murdered'.

The type of job loss that created long-term and community-focused unemployment was structural in kind and bit particularly hard in the staple industries of iron and steel, shipbuilding, engineering and textiles. Here, Britain had lost ground to competitors who were subsidising the rebuilding of their own post war economies. During the War, France, Germany and the USA had been forced to stimulate their own industry and Britain had lost valuable export markets. The Japanese took the opportunity to advance their interests, at the expense of Britain, in Far Eastern economies.

Having lost 20 per cent of her markets during the war, Britain emerged post-1918 in a much-weakened position. The staples needed investment in machinery as well as new ideas for organising production to increase productivity. But the uncertainty of the markets, the high cost of investment in research and innovation led companies to invest abroad, often to directly competing nations. The textile employers began to decamp to India. Whereas in the past, they would have produced cotton goods for export, they now exported cotton-spinning machinery to India so that goods could be imported. As the Dominions developed their own industrial sectors, they also sought to protect their embryonic production behind barriers that kept the 'parent' economy out. British interests were challenged by the revolutionary upheaval in China, which after 1927 and the massacre of the communists in Shanghai, threatened to again take on an anti-foreigner and more nationalist character. Investment that could have gone into new areas of production went abroad instead. Production suffered accordingly.

Table 15 Indices of UK industrial production; 1920-1938 (1909-1913 = 100)

	1920	1929	1938
Above-average growth industries			
Vehicles	203.7	384.4	647.6
Electrical Engineering	169.7	217.0	389.0
Gas, water, Electricity Supply	141.4	204.7	338.0
Building and Contracting	101.1	217.1	262.3
Tobacco	163.2	198.8	243.2
Food	123.2	162.6	232.1
Non-ferrous Metals	96.5	152.6	226.2
Timber and Furniture	87.8	174.1	218.2
Paper and Printing	131.4	170.6	207.2
Below-average growth industries			
Chemicals	121.0	134.0	168.5
Mechanical Engineering	104.4	132.3	142.5
Leather	86.3	107.5	125.4
Ferrous Metals	99.4	106.8	121.1
Clothing	72.2	102.4	116.2
Declining industries			
Mining and Quarrying	85.8	98.8	90.4
Shipbuilding	123.8	87.2	77.0
Textiles	97.4	86.7	100.5
Drink	96.3	82.0	92.5
All manufacturing industries	111.4	136.3	175.9
All industries	108.3	138.8	175.5

Source: K S Lomax, 'Production and Productivity Movements in the United Kingdom since 1890' (1959). The original figures are based on 1924= 100. They are re based here on 1909-13 = 100.

For Government, unemployment of a casual or seasonal nature was easier to explain. It could even be contained by using the now distinctly rusty Poor Laws, framed in 1834 [1845 in Scotland] and still staggering around through the twenties. But the kind of 'shock' unemployment that appeared in 1921, or as a result of the Wall Street crash in October 1929, which led to the Great Depression, could be neither ignored, nor so easily explained. Why? Firstly, because of the scale. Secondly, because of the speed of its appearance – between 1920 and 1921 the insured workforce unemployed rose from 3.5 to 17 per cent. Between December 1929 and December 1930 unemployment rose by nearly 40 per cent. Finally, because of its concentration in Scotland, Wales and the North. This scale and degree of concentration made it all the more visible to the public. In mining communities, for example, the stigma of being unemployed all but disappeared. Virtually everyone in such communities was either unemployed or touched by it as a result of family ties.

The wave of job loss broke all government machinery for dealing with unemployment. In 1924 and 1931, it broke the government itself. Reportage and literature of the time was powerfully shaped by the existence of deep pockets of joblessness and, at the same time, brought the issue into the open giving it mass exposure. Max Cohen wrote 'I Was One of the Unemployed', BL Coombes wrote 'These Poor Hands', Lewis Jones wrote 'Cwmardy' and its sequel 'We Live'. The focus in each case was local but the impact was national. Although concentrated in certain industrial sectors and geographical areas, the spread was national, and became evident in London and the South East too. The effects of such writing was amplified as it was drawn into reportage in the burgeoning magazine market. Advances in print technology allowed for more extensive use of photography and thrived on the kind of images used to illustrate the cover of this book.

The nationwide character of 'the dole' was brought to public attention by Orwell in his 'The Road to Wigan Pier' (1937) and much more so by Priestley in his 'English Journey' (1934). Each of these writers focused on the plight of the long-term unemployed. Despite the editorials of the Fleet Street newspapers, they demonstrated that it was primarily loss of income, which, when added to inferior housing conditions and poor health provision, formed the root cause of poverty. Where once Dickens, Booth and Rowntree wrote powerfully, exposing poverty, yet the unemployed were generally considered to have brought their misery on themselves. By the early 1930s poverty and unemployment went hand in hand. This realisation represented a dramatic breakthrough in public consciousness. Before 1914 even class-conscious workers thought the unemployed were unemployable as a result of their own inadequacies or lack of endeavour. Discovering that unemployment had real material causes, way beyond those of supposed personal characteristics, shone an even brighter light on the Government's need to act. The dynamic interrelationship of poverty and unemployment, once publicly exposed and accepted as conventional wisdom, also affected political parties, and social and welfare reformers. Would they come up with answers?

The few government remedies that had been tried would clearly not do. Old thinking lingered. Even as late as 1925, some ministers thought of unemployment as a winter phenomenon which would clear as soon as seasonal adjustments associated with summer casual work could kick in. Yet, over 10 per cent of the insured population was out of work.

This lack of understanding reflected a deeper failure of all sectors of society to recognise the change in character of unemployment post-war. For example, as late as 1923, the British Association was racked by disagreement over the nature of job loss. A majority view of the Association centred on population control. Malthusianism was laid to rest late in the UK. Yet, few challenged the Association view that Britain was overpopulated despite the recent huge loss of male adults in the trenches of France. Some, such as Dr Cornish, championed population growth and planned emigration in an attempt to reinforce the Empire.

Beveridge, President of the Economic Section of the British Association, challenged the Malthusians. Significantly, he argued that there being no evidence of an overpopulated Europe, unemployment was really a problem of industry. This was only partially accurate. Unemployment was a problem arising from the nature of private appropriation in industry and of the direction in which industry was being taken.

This dilemma faced organisations such as the NUWM, and others, who saw the root cause of unemployment but were forced to concentrate their efforts, not on the owners of capital, but on reshaping government policy. To be more accurate, the NUWM were forced away from developing a policy that could challenge the nature of ownership and direction of capital, to a position of developing policies of defence and opposition to government welfare policy. This is not surprising as the NUWM was made up, not of those in work who could be encouraged to take an interest in the direction of the capital that employed them, but of those previously employed. To make matters yet more difficult, they sought to reshape the policy of a series of governments who, throughout the inter-war years, saw no role for themselves in directing the economy away from job loss to one of job creation.

Between 1919 and 1939, three main political parties were vying for Office and each had a role in Government, separately and in combination, at some time during that period, especially through the national governments that dominated the 30s. On economic policy in relation to unemployment, there was little to choose between Conservative, Liberal and Labour. Each party subscribed to the centrality of the Gold Standard in much the same way as some today subscribe to the notion of a single currency. Even at a micro level there was often little to separate the parties. In 1929, for example, Labour included encouraging emigration, for the first time, in its programme.

The Gold Standard had been suspended during the War. To the orthodox economic strategists of all three parties, with Labour's Snowden the most combative, a return to the Gold Standard would signify a return to free trade. They believed that this was a 'natural state' for the British economy. Free trade would allow Britain to reassert her world hegemony in economic affairs and force competitors back into the market place. World trade would be reborn and unemployment disappear.

No matter how tight things got, for those orthodox thinkers, the Gold Standard would open markets. A balanced budget would reinforce confidence in Britain's economic performance. This, of course, denied three things. Firstly, that the economic pecking order pre-war and post-war had changed, with the cards reshuffled. Secondly, that the nature of unemployment had changed to long-term and structural. Finally, that capital, far from being an active agent in resolving unemployment, was a reason for accelerating it – especially when it was sent abroad! The government would have to move beyond the old orthodoxies of creating 'environments' and 'confidence', to direct intervention. It was this tension that divided economic thinking for two decades.

The Gold Standard was to be the answer to everything, a force for self-regulation and balanced books. It was believed that as governments would only be able to issue money to the value of gold reserves, this alone would act as a brake. If the economy performed well, exports would rise along with revenues. Price rises would, in turn, attract imports and governments would have to transfer gold abroad to pay for the loss of exports. This reduction in the supply of gold would force prices down, making domestic manufacture more competitive, bringing in more gold as exports began to rise again. A virtuous circle, if ever there was one, except that, as with much economic theory, it did not work in practice. A brief look at the performance of domestic exports between 1929 and 1932 illustrates the scale of industrial collapse. See Table 16.

Table 16 UK domestic exports; 1929-1932

	1929 (£m)	1932 (£m)	% Decline
New Ships and Boats	15.5	3.9	75
Non-ferrous Metals	18.3	6.9	62
Iron and Steel	68.0	28.0	59
Electrical Goods	13.2	5.8	56
Textiles	213.9	98.8	54
Machinery	59.6	30.3	49
Vehicles and Aircraft	20.7	13.3	36
Coal	52.9	34.3	35
Chemicals	26.6	18.5	30
Total Domestic Exports	729.3	365.0	50

Source : B R Mitchell and P Deane, Abstract of British Historical Statistics (Cambridge UP 1972)

In the 1920s and, even more so in the 1930s, economies were becoming more complex. The internationalisation of capital, the growing numbers competing and the internationalising of divisions of labour made quick clinical remedies impossible to apply. This did not stop Churchill, Snowden, Chamberlain or MacDonald from trying. Each followed deflationary policies in the hope that a fall in prices would lead automatically to greater competitiveness. They were oblivious to, or perhaps they deliberately ignored the fact that greater competitiveness could be achieved without more investment or increased employment.

At the same time, they were seeking to reduce government expenditure and pay off the national debt.

Table 17 UK Government expenditure (central and local); 1910-1935

	1920 (per cent)	1925 (per cent)	1930 (per cent)	1935 (per cent)
Military Defence	32.6	12.5	10.4	12.6
Social Services	25.9	36.3	42.3	46.5
Economic Services	12.8	12.3	11.6	11.2
National Debt Services	20.4	28.4	25.4	18.5
Environmental Services	1.6	3.0	3.3	3.7
Administration	4.5	4.6	4.1	4.3
Law and Order	2.1	2.8	2.8	3.0
Overseas Services	0.2	0.1	0.1	0.1
Total Expenditure (£ million) At current prices	1,592	1,072	1,145	1,117

Source: A T Peacock and J Wiseman, The Growth of Public Expenditure in the United Kingdom (OUP 1961)

Table 18 UK Government social expenditure (central and local); 1910-1935

	1910 (£ million)	1920 (£ million)	1930 (£ million)	1935 (£ million)
Education	33.5	88.8	104.2	111.7
Unemployment	a.	10.8	101.6	99.0
Poor Relief	16.1	34.2	42.5	51.8
Pensions War	a.	100.9	49.2	40.4
Pensions Old Age and Other	7.4	20.7	72.1	88.4
Health Care	4.3	44.9	58.1	63.6
Housing	0.9	4.7	40.0	48.2
Totals	62.2	305.0	467.7	503.1

Source: H M Treasury, Public Social Services (1937), Cmd 5609, pp.6-7
Note: a = not available

This inflexible policy exacerbated the numbers unemployed whilst, at the same time, benefits available to alleviate its impact were being cut. In retrospect attempts to use the Gold Standard as a fixed and unerring economic lodestar seem almost eccentric — except that a new version reappeared in the 1990s in the form of Economic and Monetary Union and the single currency. It is followed with the same lack of rigorous investigation or vision. Peter Dewey, in his 'War and Progress', puts the matter succinctly, "*In the long run, exchange rates are determined by relative international efficiencies, not the other way around. To see the Gold Standard as a solution to British inefficiency was to put the cart before the horse.*"

With the exit of the second Labour Government and the beginning of the first national Government under MacDonald, Britain abandoned it for good. But whilst the attachment to the Gold Standard had to be dropped simply because it was destroyed by the Wall Street crash, allegiance to economic orthodoxy and balanced budget, if anything, was increased. Desperate measures were taken which backfired. In August 1929, the Government were responsible for sending 8,500 unemployed miners as 'harvesters' to Canada. It quickly became apparent that the scheme was rather shabby. Miners were expected to work at below accepted wage rates and sought to return en masse to England. Labour had supported sending them.

Only inside the Liberal and Labour Parties was there an attempt to intellectually break with this orthodox, Treasury straightjacket. In the Liberal Party, John Maynard Keynes warned against the 1925 return to the Gold Standard, lashing the then Chancellor, Churchill, in a pamphlet entitled 'The Economic Consequences of Mr Churchill'. Keynes argued that Churchill's policy would benefit the banks and impede industry. After the return to the Gold Standard, industry continued to shed, on average, 100,000 jobs a year up to the Crash, whilst invisible earnings as a proportion of GNP rose steadily. Keynes was a minority voice in the Liberal Party and remained pretty much in the wilderness until the mid-1930s.

The Independent Labour Party (ILP), affiliated to the Labour Party, did subscribe to some of Keynes' views. It was developing its own economic radicalism through characters such as Mosley and John Strachey. They argued for some elementary protectionist policies to cushion those industries regrouping and retooling. Snowden dominated Labour Party economic theory. All talk of Imperial tariffs, protection, or public works and major capital project-led growth were anathema to this narrowest of orthodox free-traders. There would be no room for policies that relied on anything more than the

UNEMPLOYMENT.

SIR OSWALD MOSLEY.

SPEECH IN THE

HOUSE OF COMMONS, 28TH MAY, 1930,

ON HIS RESIGNATION.

ONE PENNY

Mosley and all of the unemployed was that this illusion formed the crux of what little there was of Government economic policy. Its champion was Chancellor Snowden, the most powerful and reactionary figure in the Cabinet. It is perhaps characteristic of Mosley, always an outsider regardless of which Party he joined, that he should choose to challenge the strongest and most intransigent Chancellor of the inter- war years, rather than work with lesser men who might have been more open to new thinking.

Mosley's main position was one quite familiar to us today: reducing the retirement age to 60; raising the school-leaving age; and developing public works schemes to clear slums, reclaim land and build roads. Just how far his views became accepted in the labour movement can be seen in the illustration used to introduce Ernest Bevin's bold plan for the creation of two million jobs. But it was radical thinking for the day. In the Memorandum, he wrote "...*Great Britain could only enjoy a standard of living capable of absorbing the great force of modern production if she were insulated from the electric shocks of present world conditions... the long-term solution to the unemployment problem was to develop the home economy behind a barrier of import controls and, meanwhile, a great public works programme should be set on foot financed by borrowing and costing £200 million over the following three years.*"

For the first time, the Government had been presented with a clear alternative to the deflationary doctrines of the Treasury and the Bank of England.

On the surface, the Mosley Memorandum represents his 'left-wing' phase. But D Lewis in, 'Illusion of Grandeur', highlights the many differences between Mosley's approach and those under-consumptionist theories then popular on the Labour left. To this left, the slump resulted from excessive savings and a way out of the slump was through measures designed to release savings by a programme of redistribution. This was similar to the theories advanced before 1914 by the radical Liberal Hobson. For Mosley, the answer lay in government intervention, not through changing policies of taxation, but directly through production. Ominously, he wanted to champion the 'common interests' of workers and capitalists against the financiers and streamline government decision-making.

Mosley took the Memorandum argument to the Labour Party Conference in October 1930 where it narrowly lost. He then decamped to a halfway house, whose fellow travellers included such a disparate group as Bevan for Labour, Strachey (who later baulked at Mosley's links with Mussolini, split from him and became a Communist), Liberals such as Sir Alfred Mond (of Mond-Turner

MY PLAN FOR
2,000,000
WORKLESS
By ERNEST BEVIN
(General Secretary, Transport & General Workers' Union)
YOU GO HOME AND REST, DAD. LEAVE THIS JOB TO ME
YOU GO BACK TO SCHOOL. I'LL LOOK AFTER THIS JOB
1d.

industrial peace) and Conservatives such as Harold MacMillan (who famously savaged Thatcher over the sale of the 'family silver'). He then graduated to form the New Party in March 1931, from which the British Union of Fascists was to emerge.

Policy towards unemployment, Parliament and democratic government begun tentatively in Birmingham, tested against Snowden, and hot housed in the New Party came to maturity in the BUF. Rejection of the New Party in the elections of October 1931 pushed it further in the direction of an extra-parliamentary stance. The BUF was formed in March 1932.

Much was to change in the 1930s as national governments were formed in the wake of Wall Street, headed by MacDonald in 1931-1935; Baldwin in 1935-1937; and Chamberlain in 1937-1940. Each of these enjoyed large majorities that gave them the opportunity to shift and absorb new thinking with enough political room to take a new direction. They each moved towards protectionism and the reduction of interest rates to encourage investment. The Import Duties Bill imposed general tariffs on imports in 1932. Yet each government continued to support a policy of balancing the budget. Britain's main competitors had no misconceptions like those promoted by the Treasury and budgetary deficits became a commonly accepted means of financing reflation during an economic downturn.

Initially, the National Government had sought to defend the Pound and the Gold Standard by cutting the pay of teachers, police, armed servicemen and civil servants and there was a particularly draconian attempt to cut unemployment benefit by 10 per cent in 1931. Even this was insufficient to hold their own and Britain was forced to abandon the Gold Standard. Instead, it was forced to shift towards a form of imperial preference in trade, encouraging closure and amalgamations of inefficient manufacturing units. One of the enduring myths of the inter- war years concerns the Jarrow march: that the unemployed got more if they asked politely, using constitutional methods. Few realise that the closure of Palmers, the shipbuilding yard that employed so many Jarrow marchers, arose from a programme of mergers which led to the formation of National Shipbuilders Securities Limited, financed by the Bank of England and operating within direct government policy and with its encouragement.

An obvious effect of the shift towards protectionism was that the pound became stabilised as a result of increased domestic demand. Interest rates were reduced to stimulate home demand; they were no longer forced upwards to sustain an artificially high value pound, locked into an inflexible Gold Standard.

2,000,000 UNEMPLOYED

1,600,000 on POOR RELIEF

THE CASE AGAINST THE "NATIONAL" GOVERNMENT

ONE PENNY

THE LABOUR PARTY

INCREASED ARMAMENTS

THE MEANS TEST

This access to cheaper money resulted in a domestic upsurge in house building and the production of consumer goods. The growth of the car industry in and around centres such as Oxford was one result of this. Arthur Exell wrote of how he joined a hunger march to London from the North, but left it to become a car worker in Cowley, where he stayed for the rest of his working life. It was only at the close of the decade and as war approached that labour was drawn into the armaments industries.

All of the campaigning of the NUWM, the behind the scenes lobbying of Beveridge or Keynes, and the street theatre of Mosley, were insufficient to spur the government into taking action to promote employment. As such, unemployment continued beyond the Phoney War. Over 200,000 mainly coal miners, were still unemployed in September 1940. Unemployment only disappeared when Hitler invaded the USSR and Churchill shifted to a policy of Total War. Interventionist economic policies did not become dominant in government circles until their rationale was forced by the advent of Total War.

Within a few years, 'interventionism' became the conventional wisdom of all parties in much the same way as free trade and the Gold Standard had been a quarter of a century before. It was a rare political consensus that did much to shape the nature of change in 1945. But in 1940, intervention was adopted, not to defeat unemployment, but to oust Hitler. Although not within the scope of this book, it is worth reflecting just how effective intervention proved to be between 1939 and 1945 and considering how it could have been deployed against poverty and unemployment between 1918 and 1939. There is a serious task here for the growing ranks of British counter-factual, 'What if?', historians.

All of this may come as a surprise to readers of this book, many of whom may assume that Labour led the way against National Government rule, arguing for nationalisation, planning, integration and deficit budgeting to fund capital works – the better to combat poverty and unemployment. Unfortunately, this was not so. Such concepts only became part of Labour rhetoric as a result of the need to prosecute Total War and thence to meet the post-1945 economic challenge of reconstruction.

It is inevitable that the Labour Party, which represented the working class both in and out of work, should be criticised on its inter-war record. During the first brief period of office, little was done and nothing learned about unemployment. As RW Hyman writes "...*for the most part, the party emerged little the wiser from the 1924 experience with unemployment and the full price of failure to grasp the inadequacies of Labour unemployment policy was not paid* until the humiliation of 1931". In 1924, it had the excuse of reliance on the Liberal vote.

Similarly, the 1929-31 Labour administration has been accused of having no policy for unemployment. Robert Skidelskey in his book 'Politicians and The Slump' notes that the second Labour Government thought about unemployment in terms of "... *a total solution — but socialism would take a long time and could not be established until the majority of people were ready for it... in the meantime the Labour Party simply did not know what to do...*".

But the policy of the Labour Government of 1929 was at odds with those of the Labour Party itself and agreed at its conferences. One pamphlet produced jointly with the TUC in 1923 called for **"The resumption of trade with Russia, the reasonable settlement of the indemnity question; the cessation of waste on military enterprises abroad; the reform of the tax system; the stabilisation of the foreign exchange and extension of international credits; and the adoption of an extensive programme of afforestation, land reclamation, improvement of the transport system, construction and improvement of urgently needed public buildings and erection of electrical power stations."**

Intervention found support beyond the ranks of organised labour, radical Liberals and Mosleyites. Progressive capitalists, grouped around Sir Allan Smith and the Industrial Group in Parliament, were calling for greater state intervention to revive trade, direct spending on construction projects and indirect spending through the extension of credit for overseas trade, lifting obstacles to trade with Russia and to those companies willing to invest in the domestic economy. Amongst the projects Smith suggested was the building of a bridge across the River Benue in Nigeria; a bridge across Sydney Harbour; electrification of the home railways and a series of capital works projects in Britain. The Government failed to rise to the challenge.

However, failure to solve a problem does not indicate lack of policy. The Labour Government did have policies, but these were little different from the 'Treasury View'. Government policy was in the hands of Snowden. Snowden as Chancellor believed himself to be acting on the highest motives of principle and intellect when he wholeheartedly endorsed The Treasury line. He held to it even when it was demonstrably not working and as a result, his policies were highly unpopular amongst Labour supporters and ruinous to the party's political prospects. This was not the first, and certainly not the last time that Labour Party conference policy would conflict with those of a Labour government and Treasury-dominated Chancellor.

The Treasury view survived for several reasons. It was firmly based on an orthodox economic theory which was not successfully challenged by Keynes until 1936; it supported the immediate interests of employers and other groups favouring wage reductions; and it placed full employment behind other economic policies such as free trade, price stability and the Gold Standard. Finally, it survived because there was insufficient unity between the organisations representing the employed and the unemployed, who, if they had combined, could have become a real force for change.

In a sense, for the workers' movement, and especially those within it who were turning their minds towards an economic critique of capitalism – those in the Communist Party, ILP, Fabians and elsewhere - unemployment was just one of the symptoms of the crisis of post-war capitalism.

In their view, at least five other interrelated factors also needed to be, and were being, analysed.

First, was the exhaustion of capital brought on by the sheer scale of the First World War. Countries had lived on their capital. Huge swathes of material wealth had been destroyed and reserves exhausted.

The geography of whole countries such as France, Belgium and Germany had been altered. Political geography had changed too. Resources that could have been directed in Britain to re-equipping docks, modernising coal, and engineering and further developing road, rail, coastal shipping and other infrastructure, had been used up or directed into other spheres of economy, especially munitions.

Secondly, the result of the war had initially broken down the international division of labour and then changed it for good. The Empire was now evidently on the decline and economists were slow to recognise the impact this would have. The post-1918 redivision of the world, especially that of Europe, brought with it new political boundaries and new tariff barriers. Britain, no longer pre-eminent in the world economy, and arguably when it came to tariffs and protection, no longer pivotal, could no longer call the shots. In these circumstances, though admittedly with hindsight, the attempt to resurrect the Gold Standard seems bizarre.

Thirdly, little recognition was then given to the economic effects of the aftershocks of war. Continuing crises created insecurity. In other countries, for example, the Ruhr debacle had profound political effects and a very real impact on the national psyche. The effect of such crises on the capitalist class in Britain was equally profound with price and exchange rate fluctuations discouraging trade and investment. As we have shown elsewhere, this factor alone increased the shift of capital investment away from Britain to more distant shores.

Fourthly, the rate of accumulation dramatically declined. By the mid-1920s, it was still only half the pre-war rate. This too diminished demand for labour and lowered productivity.

Finally, remaining resources were being locked into decaying industries that desperately required restructuring or misdirected into less productive channels. Therefore, important capital was locked, in increasing quantities, into under-performing industrial sectors – such as coal, steel, and shipbuilding and failed to embrace new emerging ones such as oil, cars and chemicals.

The Communist Party and the NUWM will always have their critics. But they each recognised an important problem. How could the workers' movement develop an economic programme within capitalism when the growth of the same movement was one of the key factors in the crisis of capitalism? In the early 1920s, the Russian Revolution was fresh in the public mind. It was a daily preoccupation of the Cabinet. Indeed, a combination of the forged Zinoviev letter and a crisis caused by failure to act against unemployment, felled the first Labour Government. Perhaps the biggest blow to confidence came as a result of the failed meeting of economists and heads of states in Genoa. Industrial strife was never far away. The constant imposition of that strife on political life; the engineering lock-out of 1922; the 1924 dock strike; the general strike in 1926; armed struggle in Ireland, all seemed to strengthen the view that the revolutionary challenge to capitalism was just that extra push away. A more realistic appraisal of the situation by these forces, what Lenin called 'a concrete analysis of concrete conditions', would surely have made them consider how that workers' movement could grow stronger within a capitalist system.

Table 19 Industrial output in Britain; 1929-1932 (1929 = 100)

per cent change since 1929	1930	1931	1932
Mining and Quarrying	- 4.9	- 14.3	- 18.7
Chemical Industries	- 5.1	- 8.9	- 2.8
Metal Manufacture	- 9.8	- 29.9	- 28.2
Engineering Industries	- 5.5	- 20.4	- 24.3
Textiles, Leather, Clothing	- 8.1	- 5.2	- 0.1
Food, Drink and Tobacco	+ 0.1	- 1.9	- 2.0
Other Manufacturing Industries	- 1.9	- 4.6	- 3.5
Building and Contracting	- 7.6	-12.7	- 17.7
Gas/Electricity/Water	+ 1.8	+ 4.5	+ 7.2
Total Industrial Production	- 4.3	- 10.5	- 10.8

Source: Feinstein, National Income, Table 112

The lock-in of resources into decaying industries consigned those working in the staples to years of misery and neglect. Politics also governed the issue of trading paths to the East. Russia, desperately in need of steel, transport, mining and agricultural machinery was cut off from trading with British companies. So she turned to Britain's main competitors, striking lucrative trade agreements with Germany and buying tractors from the USA. Few can today understand how Soviet Russia could trade with Nazi Germany in the 1930s. In fact, during the 1920s when she needed trade most, only Germany gave the Soviets much needed credit. Thus Britain lost an early opportunity to strike up a trade-based relationship with Soviet Russia that could have led to employment growth for her engineering industry. Yet the UK continued to trade with Germany up to the very day the two countries went to war.

No one party or grouping within the workers' movement was able to develop a consistent economic outlook or programme to meet these five challenges or to put unemployment at the centre of economic policy. This lack of programme or vision is perhaps the principal reason that unions and the unemployed limited their campaigns to one of pressurising the government to offset the effects of unemployment. In itself, an important approach but one which left the problem of ownership and structure of capital alone.

Just how far capital was affected by such campaigns is an important question separating historians looking at the inter-war years. Figures published

DAILY HERALD
SOVIET UNION
TRADE SUPPLEMENT

SATURDAY, MAY 23, 1925

WHAT RUSSIA COULD BUY FROM BRITAIN
By C. G. RAKOVSKY
(Chargé d'Affaires of the Soviet Union)

It is repeatedly pointed out that British exports to the Soviet Union have consisted so far mainly of so-called re-export goods; from these British merchants and British shipping derive benefit, but not British industry or the British workers.

Why is this so? Because we are compelled to buy chiefly raw materials—cotton, rubber, wool, copper, zinc, lead, etc., commodities which can immediately be turned into goods in Russia, and which can then immediately be sold in order to obtain cash for the purpose of new raw materials to be transformed into goods.

But we could, in addition, be the largest of all Great Britain's customers for such products of her industries as machinery, ships, railway material, electrical plant, etc. Only under present conditions we cannot place, as we should like to, large orders for such goods. For such transactions require the use of capital for a considerable period. And we have no free capital available.

Suppose, however, that the necessary financial facilities were provided, what would be the amount of the orders which we could place with British industrial firms? I am not speaking of the enormous future possibilities, of the great equipment which Russia will require for the full development of her natural resources. I want to speak of immediate, practical things, of the orders which Russia could place now in Great Britain to satisfy the immediate requirements of her industry and her agriculture.

During last year's negotiations we had prepared a carefully worked-out scheme of orders, which could have been placed with British firms immediately after the ratification of the treaties. But a considerable time has elapsed since then, and last years' plans have necessarily undergone certain modifications.

During my last stay in Moscow I asked the State Planning Department to furnish me with a new scheme of orders which could be placed in England, taking the new circumstances into consideration.

It is upon the results of their long and complicated work that I base the following estimate (which is, of course, not an official proposal) of the possibilities which would be at once open if the existing obstacles were removed.

Taking into consideration the immediate requirements of our industry and our agriculture, the amount of credits in goods and cash which we should require from Great Britain would amount to 811,000,000 roubles (nearly £90,000,000). These credits we do not require at once, but over a period of from three to five years, according to the nature of the enterprise. Part of these credits (565,000,000 roubles) is required for industry, another (230,000,000 roubles) for agriculture, and only about 16,000,000 roubles for transport. I should point out that the credits required for transport in connection with the oil industry is included in this last figure.

The chief point borne in mind in drafting this scheme was to ask for credits only for such enterprises as have proved profitable. This would ensure that the State would not have to bear the burden of paying interest on these credits. The term of the credits would depend upon the nature of the enterprise for which they are required; but as they are to cover a period from three to five years, it is clear that some of them would already have been repaid before the others have been advanced.

The goods for which orders would be placed include turbines, motors, boilers, machines, pipes, oil-tankers, electrical installations, etc., etc. All these we require for the development of our industry, a development which, it may be well to point out, will not be detrimental to British industry, but will, on the contrary, by increasing the requirements of our country for machinery and other goods, foster the further development of the Anglo-Soviet trade.

The credits allocated to agriculture would be used for many purposes, but primarily for the purchase of the machinery so urgently required for the reconstruction of our primitive agriculture on modern lines.

What would be the immediate results of an extension of credits and loans to Russia? The resultant development of our agriculture would help to lower the cost of living in industrial countries, and particularly in Great Britain.

The development of some branches of our industry, such as the timber and paper trades, is of importance not only to Russia, but to the whole world, for the forests of Russia represent more than half of the world's available timber resources. Only if the Russian timber industry is properly developed can it become possible to provide cheap housing on a large scale in Great Britain.

Moreover, apart from special trades, the opening up of economic relations with a population which now numbers some 140,000,000 must have an important effect in increasing world trade as a whole. From the particular point of view of Anglo-Soviet relations, the participation of British credits in Russian enterprises will bring to England not only the usual bank interests, but will provide British industry with orders and will, to some extent, bring Russian economic life into the orbit of the economic development of England. And in addition, it will bring about the settlement of political questions at issue between the two countries, which they have inherited from the past, and will create a solid basis for the development of friendly Anglo-Soviet political relations in the future.

in the 1970s show that, despite being on and off the Gold Standard, for free trade, or with a system of tariffs, the distribution of personal wealth throughout the inter-war years remained fairly constant.

For some, it was a time of growth in income; a housing boom, the flowering of urban areas and of new industries and the purchasing of new white good and cars. But it was also a time of hunger and misery for millions, including many who were working at or just above the breadline. See Table 20. Many experienced this hardship between 1918 and 1939. One historian has shown that at the height of the Great Depression, 50 per cent of the population were touched in some way by unemployment. A quite astounding figure.

Table 20 Distribution of personal wealth, England and Wales; 1911-1913 to 1936-1938 (adults aged over 25 years)

Number of estates	1911-1913 (per cent)	Shares of personal wealth 1924-1930 (per cent)	1936-1938 (per cent)
Top 1 per cent	69	62	56
2-5 per cent	18	22	23
6-10 per cent	5	7	9
11-100 per cent	8	9	12

Source: Royal Commission on the Distribution of Income and Wealth (1975)

What Did The Unemployed Do About Unemployment?

> "I, a member of the great army of unemployed, being without work and compelled to suffer through no fault of my own, do hereby solemnly swear with all the strength and resolution of my being, to loyally abide by, and carry out, the instructions of the National Unemployed Workers' Movement, with the deliberate intention of pressing forward the claims of the unemployed so that no man, woman or child suffers hunger or want this winter.
>
> Further, realising that only by the abolition of this hideous capitalist system can the horror of unemployment be removed from our midst, I here and now take upon myself a binding oath, to never cease from active strife against this system until capitalism is abolished and our country and all its resources truly belong to the people."

(Oath taken on admission to the NUWM)

Before World War I, unemployment relief was considered a local issue to be administered along lines set nearly a century before by the Poor Law Act. Between the 1880s and 1914, the general view was that it was transient. Ministers thought that unemployment rose in the winter and declined in the summer. Thus, relief was reluctantly provided to tide those affected over until better times. Relief from the poor law guardians had numerous effects. In greatly curtailing internal migration, it also perpetuated the view that unemployment was transient, to be dealt with through charity and, in localising the issue, fragmenting demands for a national system of relief. With payment of relief levied from funds raised locally, it was almost axiomatic that levels of benefit would tend towards the lowest possible – in many cases significantly lower than the wage of an unskilled labourer. But because of the local nature of allocating resources, it was possible for the unemployed to have a greater impact on levels of benefit then they could today, where rates are set nationally.

The Government had anticipated mass unemployment after the cessation of hostilities and on 25 November 1918, a Bill was passed providing a 'donation' benefit to all unemployed ex-servicemen and civilians. By March 1921, all the provisions of the Bill had been revoked.

It was in the autumn of 1920 that unemployment reached two million. The National Insurance Act of 1911 had introduced compulsory insurance against unemployment in certain sections of industry such as mechanical engineering, sand milling and shipbuilding. By 1916, a total of twelve million manual and non-manual workers earning no more than £250 per annum came under the Act.

The National Insurance Scheme, and the campaigns led by ex-members of the National Shop Stewards' and Workers' Committees, who found themselves unemployed owing to a contraction of the munitions and engineering industries, combined to break the 'parish' and 'charity' illusions that existed amongst many unemployed workers and ex-servicemen at that time.

The predominant unemployed organisations existing locally and scattered nationwide were as Local Unemployed Ex-Servicemen's Organisations. Wal Hannington, a leading wartime shop steward, who was later to become a leader of the NUWM, describes these organisations as being "*formed purely for charity-mongering purposes*". Demonstrations were organised to march the streets for the sole purpose of begging charity as a means of relieving distress.

In London, he says "*it was not an uncommon sight to see two separate demonstrations of workers marching past each other in Oxford Street or other parts of the West End, and expressing actual rivalry and opposition to one another, in scrambling to collect money from well-to-do shoppers*".

In February 1915, Prime Minister Asquith concluded a treaty with a large majority of unions affiliated to the TUC, known as the Treasury Conference, which was to "*call a truce in the class struggle during the War*". Trade union leaders pledged themselves to "*fully co-operate with the Government for the successful prosecution of the War*". This meant outlawing strikes, dilution of labour, military conscription, rising prices and virtual wage restraint. This was the negative side. The positive lay in the demonstration of the power of the Government to influence labour markets. Early in the war a Ministry of Reconstruction was formed. It intervened directly in the economy and a form of full employment was established. This was an all-time first for capitalism and the lessons were not lost amongst advanced workers.

The Munitions Act of 1915 restricted the ability of the official trade union movement to effectively advance the interest of the workers; in part, because of

HAVE YOU THOUGHT?

There are two million of us unemployed. If we were organised in the

National Unemployed Workers' Movement

we should be a mighty force.

COULD THE GOVERNMENT RESIST OUR DEMANDS for work or decent maintenance if we were all acting together unitedly?

NOT BL——Y LIKELY!

(as G.B.S. would say).

Organise for the right to work and live—JOIN UP NOW!

Membership Fee is One Penny per Week.

Fill in this Form and hand it to the Branch Steward.
I wish to join the N.U.W.M.

Name..

Address..

Employed workers, in addition to their Trade Union membership, should join the N.U.W.M. to build the Unity of Unemployed and Employed Workers.

lost flexibility resulting from a shift from local to national bargaining machinery. This inevitably led to a change in the work of the unions, putting more emphasis on a localised worker representation, based on the workplace at points of production. Numerous strikes were led by shop stewards' organisations both locally and nationally and by the end of the War, many stewards had become 'marked men'. Some of these strikes, amongst the most famous being on Clydeside where engineers campaigned for a 40-hour week, were an attempt to anticipate and counteract the threat of unemployment.

The employers were soon to have their revenge. According to Hannington, *"Unemployment washed the shop stewards' movement onto the streets"*. Many shop stewards who, for the first time during the War, had adopted the politics of trade unionism, were to adapt their experiences to the unemployment movement. As the cream of British industry and the key link in the Home Front, unemployment came as a jolt to the engineers. As a group, they were the least likely to take unemployment lying down.

Among those shop stewards was another group who had a different experience and culture and whose terms of reference pre-dated 1914. From this group, the leadership of the NUWM was drawn. Born in the closing decades of the 19th century, these industrial workers grew up in the generation of new unionism, the emergence of large-scale production and mass suffrage. They would be aware of the 'Right to Work' demonstrations and other, often violent, campaigns against unemployment. They joined the early Marxist parties such as the Socialist Labour Party which had its main base in Scotland, and the Social Democratic Federation, whose leadership was evident in the Great Dock Strike of 1889. The SDF achieved notoriety for its sponsorship of demonstrations through central London against unemployment that turned into ugly rioting with many casualties.

They would then graduate to the British Socialist Party which maintained a swathe of industrial militants who went on to become the union leaders of the 1920s and 1930s. Many, such as Inkpen, Bell, Gallacher, John T Murphy, Rothstein, Wintringham, Pollitt and Hannington went on to form, or join in the early years of the Communist Party. These are the names generally known. But they represent a generation that was replicated in every industry and locale. Indeed, the National Shop Stewards Committee Movement, strongest in Scotland and other centres of engineering joined the CP en bloc. Such workers looked neither to the church nor charity, understood the added value of workers' organisations, were streetwise and tactically very astute. The fusion of 'home front' with those who served in the trenches was a powerful

THE UNEMPLOYED
OF THE
HOLBORN UNION
WILL ASSEMBLE
On Clerkenwell Green,
AT TWO O'CLOCK
On Saturday, 1st January, 1887,

And, under the direction of the

Clerkenwell Branch, Social-Democratic Federation,

WILL THEN

March to the Workhouse
To Demand Relief.

THE STARVING POOR OF OLD ENGLAND.
Tune—"Union Jack."

Let them brag until in the face they are black,
   That over oceans they hold their sway,
Of the Flag of Old England, the Union Jack,
   About which I've something to say;
'Tis said that it floats o'er the free, but it waves
Over thousands of hard-worked ill-paid British slaves,
Who are driven to pauper and suicide graves,
The starving poor of old England!

CHORUS.

'Tis the poor, the poor, the taxes have to pay,
The poor who are starving every day,
Who starve and die on the Queen's highway,
The starving poor of Old England!

There's the slaves of the needle, and the slaves of the mine,
   The postmen and sons of the plough,

And the hard-worked servants on the railway line,
   Who get little by the sweat of their brow.
'Tis said that the labourer is worthy his hire,
But of whom does he get it we'd like to enquire,
Not of any mill-owner, or farmer, or squire,
   Who grind down the poor of Old England!
                       —*Chorus.*

Old England's a dear native land in its way
   For those who have plenty of gold,
They thieve all the land on the sides of the way,
   And heap up their riches untold;
'Tis dear to the rich, but too dear for the poor,
When hunger stalks in at every door,
But not much longer these evils we'll endure,
We the working-men of Old England!
                       —*Chorus.*

A HANDBILL WHICH SPEAKS FOR ITSELF.

combination. Each strand was influenced by revolutionary politics and served to give the NUWM a combative and offensive-minded culture. These communists, to echo the Webbs characterisation, were the most effective NCOs of the labour movement. Thanks to the work of Sue Bruley, we can add the experience of unemployed women activists, especially those from the cotton industry and, as a result of the work of Mary Davis, we recognise the contribution of women from London's East End, who first cut their political teeth in the suffrage movement.

It was only after the summer of 1921 that unemployment began to look like a long-term problem. Though few of the unemployed, including its leaders such as Hannington, display any evidence that they knew how long this wave of unemployment would last. Fewer still could imagine that the organisation they were to create would be around and active for the next twenty years.

The changing nature of unemployment, no longer seen as transient and seasonal, furthered prospects for the formation of an organisation for the unemployed. In October 1920, a number of London Mayors, including Clement Atlee, (later to be Prime Minister), and led by George Lansbury, Mayor of Poplar and later Chairman of the Labour party, demanded an interview with the then Prime Minister, David Lloyd George, to discuss the increase of unemployment in their boroughs. However they were not received and demonstrations of workers from all parts of London converged on Whitehall in protest, many wearing their war decorations. A battle with mounted police ensued, leaving a number seriously injured. This was the first episode of its kind since the war and came as a shock to many, in the land that was supposed to be 'fit for heroes'.

In the weeks following the 'Mayor's demonstration' the St Pancras Council for the unemployed called a conference of all the unemployed committees in London. It was held at the end of October 1920 in the Bookbinders' Hall in Clerkenwell, London. Delegates attending represented twelve unemployed organisations and a District Council was formed with Jack Holt as Chairman, Percy Haye as Secretary and Wal Hannington as Organiser. All three were engineers from the war industries, had been previously shop stewards and were at the time members of the newly formed Communist Party. Within two weeks delegates representing 31 London boroughs were meeting twice weekly. The charity boxes were soon to go replaced by the demand that the Government should be responsible for maintaining the unemployed. To these men, coming as they did from the war industries, there was no great mystery surrounding government intervention to resolve industrial problems. If it could be done during wartime, it could be done in peacetime too.

National Unemployed Workers Committee Movement
LONDON DISTRICT COUNCIL

MONSTER PROTEST

DEMONSTRATION

OF

London Unemployed Workers

WILL ASSEMBLE ON

VICTORIA EMBANKMENT
at 2.30 p.m., Monday, Feb. 23rd

A Deputation will proceed to the Ministry of Labour to protest against the disqualification from benefit of thousands of men and women throughout Great Britain.

GEORGE LANSBURY,
M.P.
WILL HEAD THE DEPUTATION

Unemployed Workers, Rally in your tens of thousands to protest against
Starvation

By May 1921, the number registered as wholly unemployed at the Labour Exchanges, excluding those on poor relief, reached 2,126,800. In addition to those wholly out of work, there were 1,194,200 registered as short-time workers, many of them working only two days a week. Unemployment was now a national problem requiring a national response.

At the end of February 1921, the London District Council, made up of representatives of twelve unemployed organisations, decided to co-ordinate the actions of the unemployed nationwide by calling for a conference to create a national organisation. Advertised through the pages of the 'Daily Herald' this conference was held in Hoxton, East Central London on 15 April. Eighty local organisations converged to form the National Unemployed Workers' Committee Movement. The word 'committee' which implied a federal structure and a degree of local autonomy was later dropped as the organisation came to rely more on an organised centre.

The formation of a National Unemployed Workers' Movement (NUWM) put paid to the notion of unemployment being a purely local and transient issue, to be settled by charity. Indeed, one of the real achievements of the NUWM was its ability to sustain national organisation in a milieu so localised, sector-specific and transient.

The Conference set as its principle, 'Work or Full Maintenance at Trade Union Rates of Wages'. In effect, the 'battle lines' were being drawn. But drawn lines are rarely enough and if the mammoth task that the NUWM had set itself was to be fulfilled, it had to be dealt with from the root upwards, and an unprecedented organisation built almost from scratch. One of its first moves was to take over the London district journal, 'Out of Work' and give it a national readership.

The NUWM drew its leadership from wartime engineering and its first recruits from ex-servicemen. This latter group would be the backbone of its organisation until the mid-30s. Their skills, discipline and ability to make quick decisions became essential to the national hunger marches. Each march was based on companies, sergeants, quartermasters and first aiders. Section leaders wore armbands to denote rank, though these were later removed as they too easily marked out leaders as targets for arrest. For the large marches in 1934 and again in 1936, the NUWM selected its leaders from those who had served as non-commissioned officers in the Great War. In the miners' march of 1927, at least 60 per cent were ex-servicemen. Marchers would set off army style, 50 minutes marching, then ten minutes rest.

The organisation was built as follows: branches of the movement were to be

73

1 9 3 6   NATIONAL HUNGER MARCH ON LONDON

PREPARATIONS.

In connection with the preparations for the Hunger March, it is necessary for all N.U.W.M. branches, and March Committees, to give consideration to the following points:-

TYPE OF RECRUIT.
Care must be taken to ensure that only the right type of man is recruited for the march. Men who are fully conscious of the importance of the march and who can be relied upon to conduct themselves in a manner that will reflect credit to our cause. Each recruit for the march should be made aware of the fact that the march means hardships and that no guarantees of regular food or sleeping accommodation can be given.

They must understand that it is a serious working-class activity in which they are engaged. They must be prepared to accept the discipline of the Marchers' Control Council.

PHYSICAL FITNESS.
In selecting marchers, care should be taken to see that only those who are physically fit to undertake the march should be admitted. If there is any serious doubt about a recruit, and he shows a persistent desire to march, he should only be allowed to do so if a local doctor is prepared to certify him fit.

CLEANLINESS.
The question of personal cleanliness must also be considered, otherwise it is bound to give rise to serious trouble and complaints amongst other marchers.

EQUIPMENT.
No marcher must be allowed to take the road unless properly equipped. In the main his equipment should consist of in addition to his ordinary wearing apparel, - suitable boots; overcoat; army valise; blanket; change of underclothing; plate mug, knife, fork and spoon; shaving kit, towel and soap; and other personal requisites.

RED CROSS GROUPS.
Each contingent of marchers should have a small corps of comrades who have a knowledge of red cross work, and who should wear red cross arm bands. There should be at least four first aid men for each body of 50 marchers. They should be equipped with the necessary medical supplies before taking the road.

CYCLISTS.
Three or four cyclists should be with every contingent, to act as despatch riders and to go ahead into the towns making arrangements for reception.

BANDS.
If possible, each contingent should have a small band with it, preferably drum and fife.

BANNERS.
Every group of marchers, from whatever locality they come, should have a small banner announcing the town or locality from which they come, and bearing a suitable slogan which brings out the objects of the march. Banners play a very important part, particularly in the demonstrations in the town on route.

open to all unemployed workers who wished to co-operate in the fight against unemployment and for the improvement of their conditions, and each branch was to have a legal department and a women's section. Councils, consisting of delegates from all the branches in a given area were to meet regularly to plan the activities of the movement on a district basis. The governing body of the movement was a national administrative council, consisting of delegates from all the district councils throughout Britain. This met at least quarterly, to review and co-ordinate the work of the movement and to give direction and encouragement at a national level. There was to be a head office in London with national officials, elected at each conference held annually. Or this was the idea. Bert Edwards an NUWM organiser from South East London has described the organisation of local branches as *"fairly loose and flexible"* with *"no constitution or standing orders"*.

The finances of the movement were derived from membership contributions of 1d per week, for which a system of payment stamps was introduced. The machinery of the organisation both locally and nationally was to be maintained by these funds.

This was all to be sustained by the voluntary financial contributions of unemployed people who could not even afford to feed their families, so it is a testament to the organisation that actually such a structure was maintained for twenty years. In South Wales for example in the wake of the 1926 General Strike, the NUWM became the only presence of the labour movement in an area where whole Miners' Lodges became members. As such it could draw on union funds accumulated over years of voluntary contributions from members. At other times and during hunger marches, significant funds were raised both to sustain the march and the organisation. There were also contributions from Labour Party and Communist Party members and others who were in work, but what money there was largely went to sustain the centre, speakers' tours and campaigns and there was never enough. There was scant evidence of the 'Moscow Gold' it was regularly accused of receiving by the press and when the affairs of the NUWM were finally wound up in 1946 only £32 was left.

Lack of funds was to have a significant effect on the organisation especially on its democracy and representative nature. For example at the second annual conference held at Gorton Hall in Manchester, 90 local committees sent 140 delegates yet 50 other committees went unrepresented due to lack of funds. At the third conference in Coventry 109 delegates represented 74 committees yet the NUWM had 260 affiliated at the time.

Fundamentally, the structure adopted in 1921 remained throughout the existence of the NUWM, even though it operated with varying degrees of effectiveness according to the ebb and flow of employment patterns. This consistency was possible due to the type of unemployment - that, between 1921 and 1940 was concentrated in specific geographical areas, where large numbers of workers were unemployed for long periods, in certain major trades. The dominant local political parties and churches played a similar role in supplying experienced personnel to take up organisational roles as officers.

Despite its formation as a national organisation, the NUWM (particularly in the first years of its existence) pressed for the established labour movement to take responsibility for organising and leading the work amongst the unemployed. Particular emphasis was placed on seeking affiliation with local TUCs or Trades Councils.

Demonstrations to secure this end took place and in 1921, a London to Brighton march was organised to press the Labour Party, then holding its June conference, to tackle the issue. The NUWM did not actually halt such efforts until the deterioration in the relations between the TUC and the NUWM reached a point where the latter was forced to act independently. An NUWM and TUC General Council Joint Advisory Committee on unemployment was established at the Plymouth TUC in 1923. This Joint Advisory Council drew up a six-point charter in February of the following year. It called for: work or effective maintenance; the government to assume responsibility for absorbing the unemployed; all unemployment relief to be completely divorced from the Poor Law; a reduction in the hours of work; provision of occupational training centres for the unemployed; and provision of suitable low rent housing.

There is no evidence that leaders of the NUWM expected mass unemployment to last. Consequently they spent much of their time on such campaigns. Hannington certainly wore a number of caps as national organiser of the NUWM and organiser of the metal trades section of the National Minority Movement [NMM], a militant group of trade unionists. In addition, he served as a leading official of the CP and, intermittently, throughout the life of the NUWM, as a functionary of the Profintern, at its headquarters in Moscow, and in Brussels, Other leaders of the NUWM saw a possibility of mass action over housing and against rent evictions. When funds were low as in August 1924, Hannington worked full time for the NMM.

The aim the NUWM set itself was always more than just the achievement of full employment. They had to convince both the employed and the unemployed that this could be achieved, while willing to concede that their organisation would reach a natural conclusion when that time came. This became an issue when, at the outbreak of World War II, there was uncertainty whether or not it should continue. In the end, it was kept in suspension. Even revolutionaries can hedge their bets! They had a difficult task indeed. On the one hand, to motivate the unemployed and to convince them of the necessity of struggle, they had to posit the viability of advance within capitalism. But all the time the NUWM leadership were themselves convinced that capitalism had to be broken if full employment was to be made possible.

Often convicted by their own prejudices, the NUWM worked to change the attitudes of millions, restoring their dignity, confidence and self-respect through the strenuous fight for work or full maintenance. The extent to which it achieved this is one of the yardsticks by which we must judge its merits. Richard Croucher, in his pioneering book on the NUWM 'We Will Not Starve in Silence' has gone furthest in trying to measure the impact of the NUWM on public policy, and levels of benefits as well as less tangible subjects such as changing mindsets and attitudes.

It may be possible to take this latter factor further still, though time is short as this generation is dying out. To measure the influence of the organisation, we would need to look at the origins of the NUWM and the characters that played a key role in its formation. We would need to add those who joined it in the Thirties and had their first taste of the labour movement through the NUWM. Finally we can look at those of the NUWM who found jobs and took a public awareness of social issues and unemployment into the labour movement. Many such people in the localities stayed politically active throughout their lives. When, for example, the history of the Greater London Trades Councils was written in the 1980s, a number of delegates and officers had been members of the NUWM. Some became officials of unions, local and national politicians of note and shapers of public opinion through the press and the civil service. Their impact from 1945 was considerable. Through them, Britain progressed from being a country once supposedly fit for heroes to one which would never again be a land of 'dole'. Hannington went on to become national organiser of the Engineers' Union that enshrined the 'Right To Work' in union policy. Arthur Horner became Secretary of the Miners' Federation of Great Britain and Atlee, leader of the Mayors demonstration in the early twenties and on the plinth speaking at the 1936 Hunger March rally, became the first Prime Minister of the post-war period. Bevin and Bevan, Beveridge and Keynes need even less of an introduction. Though it may be for another author at a future time, a cursory glance at cabinet concerns during the 1940s, shows very clearly how far questions of industrial and employment policy had travelled in just two decades. The strife of unemployment had done much to move thinking on such matters forward.

Of course, the NUWM could have focussed solely on the question of unemployment and unemployment benefits. Instead, it attempted to raise the issue of unemployment amongst those in work as well as those without. It dealt with housing and health problems, as well as other by-products of unemployment. It tackled government policies, opposed the rise of Mosley's Blackshirts and acted on many international issues from the 'Hands off Russia' movement and opposition to the Italian invasion of Abyssinia to the Civil War in Spain and the drift towards a Second World War in the later 1930s.

The NUWM Early Years And The 1920s

Deputations, demonstrations and the breaking up of council and boards of guardians meetings, whilst commonplace and often occurring on an unorganised basis, were symptoms of a mood that was to provide the first concrete victory for the NUWM. This was the break-up of the parish 'dole' and workhouse system. In 1921, the outcry against this system grew, forcing the Government to bear a greater responsibility in its dealings with unemployment relief, shifting emphasis from local to national.

On 30 June 1922, the Government cut unemployment benefit rates to 15 shillings for men and 12 shillings for women, a return to the rates of twelve months previously. At the same time, local boards of guardians reduced their rates of relief and offered tickets for the hated workhouse to '*heal the effects of the cuts*'. The NUWM met these attacks head on. Showing brilliant flexibility of tactic, it mobilised people not to wait for their workhouse tickets but to apply for them 'en masse' and to march on the boards of guardians and workhouses demanding relief.

In Wandsworth, over 1,000 workers and their families marched to the workhouse where only 200 places existed. The boards of guardians who administered the workhouses were forced to feed and house these people. This happened all over the country, but was most pronounced in London, in such areas as Battersea, Hammersmith and Clapham. In Wandsworth, the local authorities had been beaten by the 27th July and the guardians were forced to restore the former position of outdoor relief to all able-bodied applicants. The poor relief system was proved to be totally inadequate to meet the growing problem of unemployment. In Sheffield on 12 August in the same year, 15,000 demonstrators marched to meet the Lord Mayor to demand the dissolution of the poor relief system and won large rises. The same story can be told from Bristol... to Cardiff... to Aberdeen...

In East London and in South Wales demonstrators were often pushing at an open door with local guardians sympathetic to the cause of the unemployed, themselves lobbying central government to be allowed to pay higher rates of relief.

Hannington wrote, "*Under the pressure of our agitation the scales of relief administered by the boards of guardians were being raised almost every week*". Councillors from the East London borough of Poplar were sent to prison for being 'too extravagant' with their payment of relief. Fortunately they were released after six weeks due to massive popular pressure.

At the second National Conference of the NUWM (21-24 November 1921) a specific programme of demands and a formal structure were adopted. It was a national conference in the true sense, meeting in Manchester, and for the first time included delegates from Scotland. Constructing an organisation on the shifting sands of unemployment posed a major challenge to the delegates who went on to debate and formulate a 'structure' for the NUWM. Nowadays the modus operandi and constitutions of most labour movement organisations are a given, historically evolved, with unions increasingly homogeneous in structure. They rarely receive major scrutiny unless a merger or amalgamation is proposed. The NUWM however, was formed against a backdrop of radical change in the framework of labour movement organisations. No early leader of the NUWM would be able to guess the shape that it would take as an organisation. There were a wide variety of influences prevailing on the structures adopted by the large amalgamated unions such as the Transport and General Workers' Union then being formed. Influences such as syndicalism and guild socialism ran alongside those of the Plebs League and craft unionism. But there was no precedent for the construction of a national organisation for the unemployed.

On January 1 1921, after a year of campaigning for amalgamation and balloting, the TGWU was formed, led by Bevin and Harry Gosling. There were other significant moves towards a single general workers' union. Across industry, in print, the post office, and in engineering and steel, smaller unions were being mopped up by larger ones. Unions were breaking away from regionalism and forming truly national organisations. Each new merger, amalgamation and takeover was accompanied by conflict over which ideas would dominate discussions and influence structure and the drawing up of rulebooks. It is a tribute to those who were behind such change that it was achieved in the face of the worst economic crisis of the early twenties.

It was only a matter of time before the Trades Union Congress would be affected. New powers were to be awarded by constituent unions to a general council as a result of the 1919 rail strike. It was felt that greater co ordination was required and that the union movement's Parliamentary Committee as it existed, was not up to the job. A process of reflection was begun which produced the most radical change in union government in half a century. TUC powers over constituent unions were to be circumscribed, a move for a full time chairman of the TUC being heavily voted down. So, within a few years of the close of war, there were fewer unions, their functions and government rationalised.

The period was a time of introspection and consideration as to how best to meet the demands of members post war. The power of local, and, in the case of engineering, of on-the-job shop stewards was established. Organisations that were to be effective were those with a relatively small core of full-time officials and a relatively high proportion of resources devoted to local representation.

All this would shape the context in which militants would determine the relationship of an organisation of the unemployed to the organised and work centred trade union movement. At the same time they would be considering the best structure for an organisation of the unemployed.

The dominant forces behind the NUWM, the Communists, were themselves undecided as to the best method of industrial organisation to campaign for within the labour movement. As a new organisation within the movement and a product of a number of previously competing organisations such as the Socialist Labour Party and the British Socialist Party, they unsurprisingly inherited a number of conflicting positions. Industrial based organisation in the form of industrial unionism was one of them.

They could not draw inspiration from the Soviet Union, because in most ways, the labour movement in Britain was more mature and advanced. Lenin, it was said, modelled the organisation of his Bolshevik Party on the constitution of the Amalgamated Society of Engineers with which he became familiar during his stay in London. So they were driven to draw up a Communist position on class organisation that was drawn from British characteristics. The democracy was similar to that of the Engineering Union with its emphasis on the local and accountable. This was meant to be counter-balanced with a centralism based around full-time paid so-called 'professional revolutionaries'. It extrapolated this unhappy 'marriage of convenience' of democracy and centralism from its own Party structure and in so doing, sponsored probably the only form of organisation that could, at once, reflect the local character of unemployment, sustain an organisation on such uncertain foundations, and have a national focus.

Throughout the early years of existence the CP was going through a traumatic process of defining itself separately from the Labour Party. This process was reflected in a debate about structure and organisation that influenced the NUWM as well as the National Minority Movement [to which the NUWM was affiliated]. Both the NUWM and the NMM were affiliated to the Profintern or Red International of Labour Unions whose headquarters were first in Brussels and later in Moscow. Each was anxious to demonstrate that it subscribed to a form of organisation different from that of social democracy and therefore more militant. Put crudely, the Labour Party was an electoralist party that aimed at moving to socialism through securing majorities in the House of Commons. The CP was for mass and militant action to overthrow capitalism. Elections were a tactic. Parliament would be replaced by a British kind of Soviet.

In Britain, separateness and division of political parties were acceptable but divisions involving class-wide organisations such as unions simply did not work and never could. All CP organisations of separateness, including non-official unions for Scottish miners and a London union for tailors, were dissolved by the mid 1930s, and the only one that had any lasting significance, the NUWM, survived because it had a respectable track record.

There are a number of interesting reasons why this should be so. The first is that the organisation sought to structure itself not according to dogma and political expediency but to the life experience and requirements of the unemployed: it concentrated on local, industrial and community issues. When 'push came to shove' and the CP sought a mirror image organisation of itself for the unemployed, CP militants knew this could not work. So, whilst the organisation was, on paper, 'democratic centralist', it was in reality democratic. Most major initiatives came from the locales and were often carried over the protestations of the national 'professional revolutionary' leaders. Secondly, the leadership of the NUWM though communist, subscribed, (and indeed was often criticised by their own party for doing so), to an industrial, pragmatic and neo-reformist approach. Success or failure for the NUWM was based on its ability to secure changes immediately, no matter to what degree, in order to ease the daily lives of desperate people. The unemployed could be persuaded to revolutionary politics, and many were, but they had to put food on the table to live and where the local members were not prepared to go, no amount of head office circulars could persuade them.

Finally, as we have already seen, the ideological centre of those leading the NUWM lay with a strain of British and Labour thinking that was local, industrial and workplace based. They were, when all was said and done, both shop stewards and local ambassadors. Amongst their number, (though in true communist fashion later expunged from Party history), was Tom Quelch, son of the 1889 Great Dock Strike leader on the Thames South Side, Harry Quelch. Tom was a product of the Plebs league and a worker intellectual, excelling when it came to organisation. In the early years of the CP he wrote a number of articles and pamphlets setting out how British revolutionaries might influence the organisational structure of the trade unions. Hannington would have read this work and its influence on the structure of the NUWM is not difficult to see.

When the second NUWM conference met in Manchester, it drew up a programme that included and demanded:

(a) endorsement of the National Scale of relief (advanced at the first Conference);
(b) provision of work at rates and conditions not below the minimum laid down by the respective trade unions or, alternatively, full maintenance of the unemployed at trade union rates, where these rates did not fall below the rate demanded of the guardians;
(c) extra relief grants to expectant mothers: milk; etc.;
(d) the provision of three meals a day, weekends and holidays included, to children and unemployed parents;
(e) no rise in rents or rates for an unemployed person;
(f) the preservation of civic rights to a citizen on acceptance of relief because of unemployment;
(g) the abolition of 'test' or 'task' work for those in receipt of relief through unemployment;
(h) the free unconditional provision of halls to enable the unemployed to meet;
(i) the use of public parks and recreation grounds for public meetings;
(j) relief granted to unemployed persons to be a charge on the National Exchequer and not on the local rates, and to be administered through the trade unions;
(k) representation of the Unemployed Organisation on all Employment Exchange Committees;
(l) the abolition of all overtime in order to prevent unnecessary unemployment.

This was a programme drawn up by delegates who never considered the option that they might be long-term unemployed. Their concern was a mixture of relief for the unemployed alongside measures such as abolition of overtime

83

· WORKSHOP · ORGANISATION

The Need for Shop Committees

BY TOM QUELCH

The Trades Union Congress at Scarborough, 1925, passed the following:

> "Congress considers that strong well-organised Shop Committees are indispensable weapons in the struggle to force the Capitalists to relinquish their grip on industry, and, therefore, pledges itself to do all in its power to develop and strengthen Workshop Organisation."

PRICE ONE PENNY

:: The National Minority Movement ::
38 Great Ormond Street, London, W.C. 1

that imply an ongoing concern with industrial matters. As yet, long-term unemployment was not significant. Many delegates would therefore have retained contact with the employed and would see themselves as soon returning to work. They would also consider it a matter of time before the unemployed organisation was formally drawn into the labour movement. They were mistaken on two counts, the first being that the NUWM proved unable to find a place within official labour bodies, especially the unions. Secondly, as long-term unemployment kicked in and whole communities were made unemployed, the contact of NUWM representatives and organised, working unionism became fragile and politicised. Programmatic concerns were to become tempered by realism, focused on relief and divorced from the overriding need to get back into a job.

The initial work of the movement was debated and various tactics discussed. 'Workshops' were held on organising demonstrations, 'raids' on factories and guardians' offices, fighting against low rates of wages on relief jobs, strike solidarity with workers in dispute and different methods of halting evictions.

Factory raids became commonplace. In St Pancras for example, an engineering firm was discovered to be working regular overtime. Without consulting management or the police, a number of the unemployed 'raided' the factory and, sealing it off, proceeded to address a meeting of the workers employed there, discussing unemployment and calling for an end to overtime thus coercing the management to employ more workers. The management entered into discussion with a joint deputation of the NUWM and engineering workers and agreed to cease all overtime after Christmas of 1921. Three weeks later on 1 January 1922, compulsory overtime did cease and 40 new workers were taken on. Bert Edwards, described many years later, how, *"we would cut the phone wires, march in and take over the office, then we would call the workers to a mass meeting in the factory, get up on one of the benches and talk to them about the problem of them working overtime when there was anything up to two million unemployed."* He often got the results he desired.

At the time, it was still possible to marginally influence the extent of unemployment by intervening in local labour markets - especially those where the unemployed had worked in a factory that was still operating. But in a time of general shutdown, the effect of such local intervention declined and emphasis was shifted to national action and attempts to influence the government.

The offices of Boards of Guardians were occupied by unemployed people demanding higher rates of relief all across London and also in Scotland, with such actions often ending in violent confrontation with the police. The NUWM sought, unsuccessfully, to convince the unions that they should administer unemployment benefits rather than the poor law authorities. This was not as out of place as it may sound. A number of craft unions had done just that for generations.

Task work was a Government scheme, whereby the unemployed would be set to work but would receive no pay other than their relief. It was often backbreaking work and was hated accordingly.

As a scheme for dealing with the unemployed, it hardly got off the ground before it was dealt a deathblow by the NUWM. In both West Bromwich and Basingstoke, where work was being paid at 75 per cent of the trade union rates, unemployed workers marched to the sites where task work and relief work were being carried out, confiscating shovels, pickaxes and hammers. They then marched to the offices of the district surveyors in the respective town halls where they unceremoniously deposited the tools! The work did not go ahead.

Solidarity actions were organised in this period, especially around the four months' lockout in the engineering industry. In Rochdale in December 1921, many members of the NUWM were arrested for organising against scab labour during a railway workers' strike and in 1923 and 1924 the unemployed joined the picket lines of striking dockworkers. The first strike was against a wage cut and the second for a wage rise and each was supported by the unemployed organisation.

In many ways, the unemployed, having appeared on the social and political scene, as a new force in big numbers, were an unknown factor. It was difficult to foresee how they would behave en masse. Their grievances were many and obvious and most had seen service during World War One and were inured to a militant life. Until the NUWM appeared, unemployed actions, involving a great many men wearing their colours and decorations, were unpredictable. The actions of the unemployed throughout the 1920s were accompanied by a good deal of violence, though to their credit, looting was very rare. Only in the mid-1930s did the violence, visited on unemployed demonstrations, tail off.

Unsurprisingly, there was general concern amongst some unions that the unemployed might be used as blacklegs in strikes and as cheap labour undermining local wage agreements. The NUWM worked energetically to combat this, famously earning the gratitude of Ernest Bevin for supporting the dockers' strike of February 1924.

The NUWM also campaigned consistently for higher rates of unemployment benefit and work at trade union rates. This constant tension between representatives of the unemployed and the employed in union membership was never adequately resolved. In 1924 for example, the TUC Congress rejected a proposal whereby members of the NUWM would automatically transfer membership to the appropriate union if they got a job. Probably the reverse option implicit in this proposal put them off. Some in the TUC, suspicious of communist leadership in the NUWM, did not want their members transferring out into a CP-led organisation. Instead they began to think of establishing organisations for the unemployed that could rival the NUWM, keeping them within their own control. A number of smaller unions, unable to wield influence within a TUC that was increasingly dominated by new, larger amalgamated unions, were comfortable with their relationship with the NUWM. Within the TUC they pressed to formalise a relationship between it and the NUWM. Even as late as 1926, the national headquarters of the NUWM was dependent on donations from unions such as the furniture makers.

The Second National Conference had also charged the unemployed movement with resisting the evictions that were commonplace amongst them. In South York Street in Glasgow on 17 May 1921, thousands battled with police to halt the eviction of three unemployed families and the Glasgow City Council was forced to set up a special rent fund to relieve tenants who were in danger of such eviction.

On Armistice Day, 11 November 1922, a huge demonstration took place at the cenotaph. Some 35,000 ex-servicemen in London displaying medals and pawn tickets marched to highlight the plight of those still searching for "the land fit for heroes". This march had a great impact in highlighting the poverty of unemployment and the extent of its existence.

Attitudes towards unemployment and the unemployed were changing on a large scale and in a short period of time. The NUWM, nationally, through its initial activities, had roused many hundreds of thousands from their acceptance of the inevitability of poverty and unemployment. Commenting on the Cenotaph march, Hannington wrote "They (the demonstrations) were now different from those that had taken place a year previously. The collecting-box practice had been ended and the unemployed marched, not as beggars, appealing for alms in a servile manner, but as spirited class conscious men and women, demanding justice from the Government for their grievances as unemployed".

The words 'spirited' and 'class-conscious' whilst not being overstated should not be forgotten. These were the men and women who went on to take part in the hunger marches that did so much to destroy the workhouse system. For an organisation without precedent, the NUWM had, in a few years changed both the basis and direction of unemployed campaigning and had also illustrated the potential for change that existed in that section of the population. The NUWM were the embodiment of the interests of the unemployed and acted as their spokesmen. They did not have a monopoly on the issue of unemployed representation as it was not unusual for trade union leaders to talk about the need for a one-day general strike against unemployment to convince the Government of the need to tackle the problem. Indeed, the idea was widely, if not successfully, canvassed in the pre-general strike period. But as organisers of the unemployed, the NUWM had a virtually open field.

In the opinion of the unemployed, many of whom were trade unionists, the future lay in the solid foundation of the organised labour movement so this period where the NUWM gathered its initial support cannot be underestimated. It was the initial work of the NUWM that gave it the strength to continue its struggle right up to 1939, even when one of its strategic potential allies, the TUC, failed to agree the necessary unity of action.

During the period before the General Strike, with the absence of rival organisations and given that unemployment was a major issue, the NUWM, both in its policies and activities, was accepted as a component in the mainstream of the labour movement. But its relationship with union officials was prickly. Throughout its existence, the organisation hovered between being 'official' and 'unofficial'. In the 1930s, for example, when NUWM organised hunger marches were disclaimed by the TUC General Council, the Labour Party, as well as many constituent unions and trades councils approved them, often enthusiastically.

Though a young and relatively small organisation throughout the 1920s, the number of people mobilised was far in excess of its membership. In its local, district and national leadership were a good number of seasoned workers with an exceptional capacity for organisation and campaigning, often in the most adverse situations. But its attempt to stake a claim to an official place in the labour movement was frustrated, particularly after the General Strike in 1926, when conflicting views on many major issues split the working class movement. In some ways, the 1926 strike was a hollow victory for the employers who, in a desperate attempt to break the miners, ended up laying whole parts of the country to waste; but it drove a wedge into a labour movement unsure as to how they should respond. The NUWM lost no time in allocating blame and did little to heal any rift.

Employed And Unemployed Unity

> "This terrible unemployment which we are seeing today cannot be solved by legislation"

From the speech by King George V, Opening Parliament in 1921

Britain was the first country where workers had learned the meaning of combination and unity in order to survive the conditions that existed during and after the Industrial Revolution. Unity was a factor that was etched deep in Union consciousness.

Other than trade, craft or industry working class organisations in Britain divided neither politically, regionally, ethnically or on the basis of religion. There was one trade union centre, the Trades Union Congress, under whose banner marched all organised labour. All disagreements and political divergences were accommodated and resolved within the family of Labour.

In the 1920s, the large number of unions meant that a much greater proportion of their thinking and time was given over to inter-union disputes and to this disunity was attached the stigma of strikebreaking and class collaboration. Into this minefield stepped the organisation of the unemployed.

All attempts at setting up rival, parallel or separate organisations in opposition to the established trade unions, were to come to nought. From whatever part of the political spectrum they came, be it the Syndicalists and Shop Stewards' Movement, the rival Miners' Unofficial Unions, established in the late twenties, or even those of Mosley's BUF, parallel unionism never took hold. Though not a favoured member of the family of Labour, the NUWM followed its historic path, embracing all unemployed regardless of gender, religion or political belief. Sometimes its leadership found the latter category a difficult one to embrace but where it failed it paid a price.

Whilst the issue of unemployment was not new, the NUWM, from its formation, found itself organising in a vacuum where few unions dared or wished to tread. Most craft unions were either winding down arrangements such as journeying and tramping that had traditionally spread the load of unemployment. They had not been able to sustain funding of programmes to encourage emigration beyond the first twentieth century wave of unemployment between 1905-08 and funds for the relief of unemployed members quickly dried up. Where the protagonists of new unionism in the 1880s had characterised craft unions as 'coffin clubs', by the 1920s all types of union were failing to deal with unemployment.

Furthermore, organising the unemployed presented difficulties of quite peculiar complexity. In the first place, the psychology of those unemployed was quite different from that of the employed – they did not see themselves as belonging permanently to that category and therefore were inclined to give only tepid and wavering allegiance to the unemployed organisation. It is not easy to give organisational expression to circumstances from which men are trying desperately to escape. At first, joining an organisation of the unemployed seemed to many a virtual acceptance of their lot, a sort of abandonment of social status. For this reason, the NUWM sought to build a close relationship between unemployed and trade unions. Segregation can create thought patterns in the minds of the unemployed that insulate them from the rest of the working class. This only changed when the unemployed became so numerous between 1921 and 1939, that they virtually constituted communities of the workless. The NUWM can be seen then as a community as well as a labour organisation.

The members of the unemployed army changed from time to time, particularly in the years immediately following the Great War. Those that remained unemployed all the time did not represent a cross-section of the working class, but tended to become an isolated social phenomenon. In this area, the NUWM had to change the nature of its work to meet peculiar needs and in some cases with workers unemployed for long periods and unions all but collapsing, the NUWM became the labour movement in the locale.

Table 21 Trade union membership and rate of unemployment; 1920-1939 (thousands)

	MEMBERSHIP	RATE OF CHANGE		UNEMPLOYMENT
1920	8,438	1920-1	-20.55	7.9
1921	6,633			16.9
1922	5,625			14.3
1923	5,429	1922-5	+2.12	11.7
1924	5,544			10.3
1925	5,506			11.3
1926	5,219			12.5
1927	4,919	1925-8	-12.71	9.7
1928	4,806			10.8
1929	4,858			10.4
1930	4,842			16.1
1931	4,614	1929-3	-9.59	21.3
1932	4,444			22.1
1933	4,392			19.9
1934	4,590	1933-9	+43.39	16.7
1939	6,298			10.5

Source: G A Phillips - The General Strike – The Politics of Industrial Conflict (1976)

The official trade union attitude towards unemployment was for many years characteristically empirical.

Initially, it had few apprehensions: unemployment was but a passing phase, an incident of post-war industrial dislocation. Even NUWM leaders such as Hannington and Syd Elias, became involved with the unemployed because they were 'natural-born' organisers. They never imagined that the numbers officially unemployed would not go below one million for the next two decades. This view of unemployment as transitory ruled out a strategic policy both in respect of the obligations of the unions to their unemployed members and to the wider aspects of economic and social policy. Some of the unions attempted to render service to their unemployed membership but were often very slow to respond. The craft unions were obliged to under rule and constitution. They, at least, had some experience of trying to regulate employment levels. Yet the extent of unemployment meant they could not possibly hope to maintain numbers of apprentices when whole trades were being put on ice. Others washed their hands of them as soon as their union membership lapsed. See Table 21. This was especially true of the larger general unions, whose members, often poorly paid, were used to casual and seasonal work. It was always assumed that such workers would surrender their card when the job was finished and pick it up again when they found new employment. Union dues were deliberately kept low in recognition of this high level of turnover, both in employment and membership. The position changed dramatically when the nature of unemployment became more general and structural. It took the unions many years to realise the folly of their position, though, arguably, the issue remains under-explored and unresolved to this day.

The biggest failing was the union's failure to grasp, and the NUWM's inability to convince, the employed that the responsibility for combating unemployment lay with those with a job. The NUWM was, as an outsider, unable to mobilise the employed workers and their trade unions to fight job losses and to call for shorter hours and more apprenticeships. This inability to motivate employed workers was to be the undoing of the NUWM and was always its major source of weakness. It was unable to convince the employed because too many still accepted that a job was a gift bestowed in good times by employers and taken away in bad. The concept of a 'Right to Work', a philosophical as much as a practical demand raised by the Engineers' Union in the 1950s, was still decades and a war away. It was a product of a quite different and far stronger union movement than existed in the inter-war years.

Before 1920, there had been two short spells where the unemployed had organised to improve their lot. There were demonstrations, often very large, throughout the 1880s and 'Right to Work' activities in 1905-1908. Generally, these actions were organised by the Social Democratic Federation and ex-servicemen's organisations, again with only nominal support from the trade unions.

By 1921-22 unemployment existed on a massive scale with a rise from 3.9 per cent to 16.9 per cent of the insured working population in one three month period. Many working class families were affected in one way or another. Few understood the causes of the slump and millions feared its consequences.

Between the Septembers 1921 and 1922 – the number of workers in unions affiliated to the TUC dropped from 6,417,910 to 5,128,648, an average monthly loss of 110,000. Constant hunger and abject poverty were the great fear of the working class. By the end of 1922, with the defeat of the engineers and the miners 'Great Lock-Outs', the employers had become stronger and pushed forward with their programme of rationalisation.

Initially, it seemed that the NUWM would be welcomed into the labour fold. The period up until the first Labour Government in 1924 was one of relatively harmonious relations between the Communist Party (CP) and other official sections of the labour movement, with many CP members also members of the Labour Party attending, speaking at, and taking a direct involvement in its affairs. Some open Communists such as Shapurji Saklatvala (Battersea) served as Labour members of Parliament. Prominent Communists were openly involved in organising the NUWM. This early period of harmony had material roots in the unity that the NUWM had shown with trade unions in organising against blackleg labour during strikes. In 1924, after the February national strike by dockers for higher wages, Ernest Bevin, General Secretary of the Transport and General Workers' Union, sent a letter to the Secretary of the NUWM that read:

"Dear Sir
I am directed to convey to you the best thanks of the Dockers' National Delegate Conference for the splendid and valuable assistance rendered by your organisation during the recent struggle.

The Conference felt that the action of your movement helped considerably in effecting a quick victory."

How far this unity existed is difficult to ascertain. A number of factors contributed to a peaceful coexistence between 'officialdom and unofficialdom' in the period before 1926. Firstly, many of the leaders of the NUWM were staunch trade unionists and had been active, particularly in the shop steward movement during their periods of employment and thus still retained their contacts and support in trade union circles; also because they were often craft workers, these NUWM members were able to retain their union cards and attend branch meetings. Secondly, the original policy of the NUWM was that the trade unions should retain their members within their organisation through periods of unemployment, and that the Labour representatives would work in Parliament to secure a political solution to unemployment. Meanwhile, the NUWM would be an affiliated to the TUC, responsible for organising those of the unemployed who had never had a job or a union card. The NUWM were seen therefore as advocates of trade unionism in general, rather than a particular brand of it.

Certainly there were some in the official trade union movement and on the

TUC General Council who were sympathetic to this view. However, there were those who were not. In 1923, GDH Cole said at the Labour Party Conference that *"Not a few trade unionists are reluctant to foster separate movements of the unemployed"*. Dukes of the General and Municipal Workers' Union said at the 1923 Trade Union Congress, *"the unemployed should be covered by the unions themselves... a separate organisation can only work to the detriment of the Trade Union Movement generally"*.

The Communist Party was campaigning at this time for affiliation to the Labour Party and their political trajectory, which held sway in the NUWM, was one of support for the Labour Party and the TUC General Council *"so long as these bodies took the working class forward"*. This attitude was to change after the General Strike when class struggle was replaced with class compromise. Between the Sheffield and Stoke conferences of the NUWM, 1924 and 1925, membership grew as did the work of solidarity with employed workers. Hannington took the opportunity, in the Communist Press, to make the case for unions to retain their members when made redundant, and for those not in a union, to be gathered together in one unemployed workers' organisation. This position received a welcome in some quarters but the 'Nine Days in May' changed everything.

In addition, we must remember that the trade union movement was reeling under the lockout defeats and was therefore too weak and too divided to organise the unemployed. The only organisations thought fit by the TUC to take on the job were the trades' councils. In Bristol, Coventry, Leicester, Macclesfield and Guildford, for example, the trades' councils had already started organising with some success. They were themselves outside the official trade union movement and, not being affiliated to the TUC, could not be influenced by or representative of general TUC policy. They did in fact group together many local activists who were sympathetic to the unemployed and to the NUWM.

January 7th 1923 was the first national day of protest and demonstration against unemployment that involved the whole labour movement. Following the success of this 'Day of Action', representatives of the NUWM met the TUC Unemployment Sub-Committee on 24th January, to discuss proposals aimed at creating greater unity between the employed and unemployed. Disagreement existed from the beginning. The most important proposal had been *"that the TUC circularise trade unions and trades councils, encouraging the formation of unemployed committees in every locality, attached to the NUWM"* and that *"At the next Trades Union Congress, the affiliation of the NUWM to the TUC should be placed on the agenda"*.

In reply, the Sub-Committee stated *"We cannot recommend to the General Council this proposal, as we consider that all unemployed workers are or should be represented at the Trade Union Congress by the properly constituted trade union bodies affiliated, and we are opposed to the principle contained in proposal No. 3 (NUWM affiliation to the TUC) as likely to lead to dual representation at the Congress"*.

At the Plymouth Trades Union Congress held in September 1923, a Sub-Committee report was adopted that provided for the setting up of a Joint Advisory Council (JAC) to co-ordinate activities. On the 10th of January 1924, this body proposed a course of action based on an Unemployed Workers' Charter containing six major points. These were: raising the scales of benefit to a standard of effective maintenance; ending the poor law relief administration for the unemployed; large-scale government work schemes at trade union rates of wages; reduction in the normal working week to help absorb the unemployed into industry; occupational training centres to be set up by the Government; and a vast new housing programme with lower rents.

A National Day of Demonstration against unemployment 'Unemployed Sunday' was called by the TUC and NUWM for the 1st June 1924 and all TUC unions were mobilised. Of this day Hannington says *"We witnessed a mighty display of working class strength. In almost every town, tens of thousands of employed and unemployed marched together under the banners of the trade unions, Labour parties, co-operative guilds and the NUWM branches"*.

In September 1924, at the Trades Union Congress in Hull, the National Union of Distributive and Allied Workers tabled a resolution in support of NUWM affiliation to the TUC. It was defeated.

At the 24th Annual Conference of the Labour Party held in London in October 1924, MacDonald and Snowden who led the first Labour administration, came under heavy fire for their failure to deal with the problem of unemployment in any depth. At the 1st June demonstration, Ben Tillett, renowned leader of the TUC, had said in his speech that *"the Labour Government is out-Torying the Tories"*. Little was done to alleviate unemployment save the setting up of a number of work schemes and a small increase in benefits. The Labour Government was badly defeated at the polls in October 1924. Throughout the lifetime of the Government, the number of strikes had grown in industry, though they were largely unofficial as union leaders were fearful of embarrassing those in power.

Another successful joint demonstration was held on 1st June 1925, this time aimed at a Conservative Government. Because of its success, the General

Council of the TUC and the Executive Committee of the NUWM decided to convene a special National Conference on Unemployment for 24th July at Central Hall, Westminster. Whilst future events have often been cited to explain the breakdown of relations between the TUC and NUWM, perhaps the most important event occurred at this Conference. The NUWM proposed the calling of a 24-hour general strike against unemployment, to be directed by the TUC. Of the 200 unions called upon by the TUC to consult their members as to whether or not they should strike, only one union complied. The result of this ballot was 32,368 in favour of a strike with 4,369 against. As only one union had conducted a ballot, it was inevitable that the TUC General Council would reject the strike proposal – despite the fact that many members of the Council, including Walter Citrine, were sympathetic.

This was not an outright TUC rejection of the NUWM but it was certainly indicative of their different ideas on the way to combat unemployment. As the breach grew wider between the TUC and the NUWM, the argument between 'militancy' and a 'reasonable approach' grew more pronounced. Each organisation began to withdraw to fixed and less flexible positions.

In the same July as the unemployment conference, the employers renewed an offensive to lower wages. The crisis in the privately owned mining industry came to a head, with coal owners issuing an ultimatum to the miners to accept wage cuts and district bargaining in place of their national agreement. In the face of a general lockout the TUC and, in particular, the railway and transport unions rallied to the miners, forcing the Government to intervene at the eleventh hour, with a nine-month coal subsidy. But the die had been cast.

From the onset of the crisis in the mines, a division was developing within the ranks of the labour movement. In September 1925, the existence of an Organisation for the Maintenance of Supplies (OMS), through which the Government would seek to offset the effects of a General Strike, was publicly announced. The TUC knew that a clash of great magnitude was inevitable, although they wished to delay the day. Generally, there was little preparation for the struggle on the part of the General Council. Of the NUWM proposal for a 24-hour general strike, Citrine, Assistant Secretary of the TUC, had said "I had hoped it would be accepted because it would have tested our trade union organisation for a more prolonged general strike if it ever became necessary to use it in an industrial dispute".

The General Council was fearful and unprepared and the NUWM were moving closer to those forces advocating a General Strike in defence of the miners. This was particularly so after Baldwin, the Prime Minister, had said he agreed with the mine-owners and thought that *"All the workers in this country have got to accept a reduction in wages"*. The NUWM identified themselves with the policy of the Communist Party and the National Minority Movement (NMM). The NMM was a grouping of left wing forces inside the major unions formed in August 1924; its main strength lay in the mining, metal work, transport and building unions. Part of its programme stated that *"the TUC General Council must give united leadership in the struggle against the employers with the ultimate object of workers' control in industry"*. Wal Hannington, Organising Secretary of the NUWM, was also the Organising Secretary of the metal workers' section of the NMM. A banner strewn across Battersea Town Hall at the Second National Conference of the NMM in August 1925 read 'Prepare for the coming fight'. At a later Special National Conference, Tom Mann (honarary treasurer of the NUWM) said in his chairman's address, *"Fully admitting that there is no real cure for unemployment under capitalism still it is quite possible to pursue a policy of increasing control of industry by the workers....This meant pressing urgently for a reduction in working hours to absorb the workless."*

Before the general strike took place, events occurred which were to ensure no further official collaboration between the TUC and the NUWM for the rest of the latter's existence. The Communist Party voiced criticism of the conduct of the 'collaboration' of the General Council with the Labour administration of 1924 and unity now existed only superficially at national level between the NUWM, the TUC and Labour Party. However, at a local branch level, particularly in South Wales, Scotland and the North, limited work between the organisations had been common. Even this was soon shattered.

The general strike affected the NUWM in a number of ways. Its offices were raided and its propaganda, records and membership lists confiscated. Many of its leaders were imprisoned, including Hannington who was one of twelve leaders of the CPGB arrested before the strike, on charges of seditious libel and incitement to mutiny, an Act dating back to 1797. Hannington served the second of five prison sentences he was to receive as leader of the NUWM. Wal Hannington later said..."*The right-wing leadership of the Labour Party and the unions did not want to fight the Government. They decided to fight the Communists instead"*. At the September 1925 Labour Party Conference, held in Liverpool, a decision was carried amidst great opposition, to expel all Communist Party members from individual membership of the Labour Party and to bar them as elected trade union delegates to local and national Labour Party conferences. It was block voting by some unions that decided the vote.

National Minority Movement
ROOM 14 (FIRST FLOOR)
38 Great Ormond Street : London : WC1

Special National Conference of Action

Chairman's Address

LATCHMERE BATHS
BATTERSEA LONDON
ON MARCH 21 1926

SOLIDARITY SPELLS SUCCESS

The animosity this decision created was widespread. The 'united front from below' policy, followed by the British Communist Party and coined by Zinoviev at the 1923 congress of the Communist International that was supposed to be directed against the capitalists became a united front from below against the Labour Party and TUC leaders. The already sharp division was accentuated by the defeat of the General Strike and a TUC failure to come to the aid of the miners who were now out on a limb.

The dissolution of the TUC-NUWM Joint Advisory Committee by decision of the TUC General Council after the General Strike was, according to the NUWM leader, part of *"the new policy of Mondism, peace in industry and co-operation with the capitalists"*. The General Council of the TUC stated it was no longer *"satisfied as to the bona fides"* of the NUWM. This was hardly surprising as its leadership consisted of those now subject to a blacklist barring them from Labour membership. The split in official terms was irrevocable. The catalyst for the split, if one were needed, was TUC endorsement of the Blanesburgh Committee Report – condemned by the NUWM. The Committee had TUC-appointed representatives, led by Margaret Bondfield, thus its endorsement of the Report became automatic. Many were surprised at the Report's key proposals: the employed to pay lower insurance contributions; benefit extending beyond the 26 week period allowed, to become transitional; and the 'Not Genuinely Seeking Work Clause' to be operated more stringently. Hannington estimated in his reply to the Report that 250,000 would lose their benefit. He was not far wrong. The division it caused left very few fences that could be mended. However, confusion, unity and disunity, all co-existed within the branches of the Labour Party and trade unions as their loyalties stretched between the unemployed and their respective executives.

The second great Hunger March of 1927, intended principally to highlight the plight of the miners, whom many thought had been disowned by the TUC, clarified the position. Citrine thought the march arose, not from *"a genuine desire to ventilate the grievance of unemployment, but rather to break the back of the official movement and to show the movement was indifferent to the claims of the unemployed"*. He proposed that all TUC affiliated organisations should boycott the march, which was, in fact, an unofficial success. The miners, many still unemployed in the wake of the strike, continued to fill out the ranks of the NUWM. This meant that, despite the official boycott of the NUWM and its activities, it still commanded support in the Labour movement. Yet dreams of official unity between the NUWM and the trade unions were now shattered. From here on, the NUWM was independent, having been all but excommunicated.

THE MARCH OF THE MINERS

How we Smashed the Opposition

By
WAL. HANNINGTON

Foreword by
A. J. COOK

Price 2d.

(With 11 Illustrations)

Published by the
N.U.W.C.M., 105 Hatton Garden, London, EC1

From The General Strike To The Great Crash

How did the Labour Party, TUC and Communists come to terms with the General Strike defeat? It affected each of them in different ways.

For Labour, the General Strike was more a concern of the industrial wing of its movement. The TUC came reluctantly into the strike fearing it could develop an insurrectionary character and a challenge for power. But it was clearly defensive in character. As the strike ran its course, it did not, therefore, raise constitutional questions that would have forced Labour to see it as anything more than a major clash between Government and unions.

The clash, presaged by a series of lock-outs, false starts and practice runs, was one the unions wanted over and done with as soon as possible after it became clear that the Government meant business. The General Council were constitutionalists and saw the strike as being played according to the rules and rituals of labour disputes that emerged between 1890 and 1914. If anything, it was the Government that did not play by the rules. The General Council entered the strike partly because it wanted to publicly express its support for a fair deal for the miners and also because of the tripartite alliance agreement of mutual support signed between its big battalions: rail, coal and transport. The miners were running ahead of their fellow unionists.

But the defeat of the strike had implications for all workers and all trade unionists. Employers in all sectors took the opportunity to sack active unionists and diminish labour. In coal it was undeclared war and wholesale closure with miners on lockout for nearly a year. So, after 1926, the General Council no longer concerned itself with the plight of the unemployed but instead attempted to hold together its own house, which was in a state of collapse. Given its reluctance to start the strike, its swift cave-in and the pressure experienced through membership loss, it is unsurprising that the General Council sued for industrial peace in the shape of the Mond-Turner talks. One thing is sure. The TUC were determined never again to embark on such a course. They have only come near such a decision once since, as a result of the

101

imprisonment of the Pentonville dockers in 1972. Even during the miners' strike in the mid-1980s the TUC strenuously and wisely avoid enlisting the whole of organised labour to fight the battle of a single constituent. After the strike, union militancy and strike activity dropped dramatically. See table 22.

Table 22 Workers directly and indirectly involved in disputes and the number of days lost; 1920-1939

YEAR	WORKERS	DAYS LOST	YEAR	WORKERS	DAYS LOST
1920	1,932,000	26,568,000	1930	307,000	4,339,000
1921	1,801,000	85,872,000	1931	490,000	6,983,000
1922	552,000	19,850,000	1932	379,000	6,448,000
1923	405,000	10,672,000	1933	136,000	1,072,000
1924	613,000	8,424,000	1934	134,000	959,000
1925	441,000	7,952,000	1935	271,000	1,955,000
1926	2,750,000		1936	316,000	1,829,000
1927	108,000	1,174,000	1937	597,000	3,413,000
1928	124,000	1,388,000	1938	274,000	1,334,000
1929	533,000	8,287,000	1939	337,000	1,356,000

Quoted in G A Phillips 'The General Strike : The Politics of Industrial Conflict' (Wiedenfeld and Nicholson 1976)

The communists only saw what they characterised as betrayal, all about them. They began a descent from being grudgingly accepted as a sort of militant conscience of Labour to becoming a pariah. If Labour and the TUC were out to make scapegoats of the communists, the 'third period' Communist policy was hardly that of a party playing hard to get.

The 'new policy' was in fact imposed on the Party by its parent organisation, Comintern during its ninth plenary meeting in February 1928. Belying the traditional historical view of communist subservience to Moscow, the new policy was first, publicly rejected, and then its implementation resisted for a number of years. Pollitt's view was expressed in The Communist in December 1928, "We describe the Labour Party as a third capitalist party. If that means anything at all, it is that our strength will grow in the degree that we can weaken the Labour party." But other leaders, such as general secretary Albert Inkpen, Comintern Executive member, CPGB delegate and west London engineer Jack Murphy and miners' leader Arthur Horner opposed saying that the Tories continued to be the historic and main force to be defeated.

Crimes Against the Unemployed

An Exposure of the T.U.C. Scab Scheme and the Crimes committed against the Unemployed by the T.U.C. General Council

By
WAL HANNINGTON
National Organiser, N.U.W.M.

PRICE: ONE PENNY

Published by the National Unemployed Workers' Movement, 35 Great Russell Street, London, W.C.1. Printed by Watford Printers Limited, 58 Vicarage Road, Watford, Herts.

The minority grouping came to power in the summer of 1929 with Pollitt replacing Inkpen as general secretary in August. The policy was disastrous for the party in many ways. Despite the level of capitalist crisis, the CPGB electoral strategy reduced it to ignominy. During the 1929 election, which was fought out largely on the basis of unemployment and economic policy, the party achieved 50,000 votes despite fielding candidates in 25 constituencies. This was less than a third of the expected figure and contrasted sharply with the 41,000 achieved in 1924 in only six constituencies. Significantly, party support plummeted in areas of high unemployment such as Battersea and Aberdeen where the organisation was a dominant working class force. Where the CP achieved affirmation of a half per cent of voters, Labour secured six million. In late 1931 only 37 per cent of its members were recorded as being in a trade union and only 48 factories had party branches in the whole country. One Comintern analysis of British party membership estimates that in June 1931, 75-80 per cent of the membership was out of work. Many of the new recruits joining in the wake of the Crash were also unemployed. Significantly, the national Hunger March of 1930 was the smallest of the inter-war years attracting only 350 participants.

Although now removed from office, or in the case of Andrew Rothstein, actually banished to the USSR, those opposed to the new line held the ground and the forces of labour movement unity prevailed within five years. Even the new leadership must have known something was wrong, writing in the Communist Review in August 1930, "*although we have stood on the line of the Comintern...yet the membership continues to fall and the Party is largely isolated from the masses.*" Perhaps there is more to the view of those who see in the 'third period' one of those doctrinal differences that arise in politics when organisations make a transition from one generation to another. In that sense the third period was as much a ruse for one group to unseat another in the leadership of the Party. Pollitt, leader of the 'third period' communists called for the postponement of the introduction of the Daily Worker. Yet opposition to the establishment of a daily was the main criticism levelled at those on the so-called right of the party.

In communist circles the 'third period' was a phase of post-war capitalism in which the working class was characterised as being held back by Labour 'mis-leadership'. True, Labour and the TUC were stepping back in the wake of the miners' defeat; but were they stepping back forever? The CP condemned Labour as 'a third capitalist party' and the TUC 'Lieutenants of capital'. Was a call for workers not to vote for Labour in the 1929 election the way to stop the retreat?

The secretive nature of the CPGB with its cell-like structure and centralised 'democracy' has, until recently, allowed historians a rather superficial answer to these questions. In general they saw the CP approach as collective suicide and a squandering of all their political gains in the early 1920s. Yet, three factors persuade us to take a closer look. Firstly, it is wrong to see only a single unified CP policy. There was much disagreement within the party over the 'third period' policy and many members left rather than implement it. Membership of the organisation fell to an all time low and indeed, the policy was quickly proven to be a dead end, jettisoned within three years in favour of a more inclusive approach and an attempt to reinvent the 'unity' days. Secondly, of all the front and mass organisations in which the CPGB played a central role during this 'third period', only the NUWM kept up or increased membership. The League Against Imperialism and International Labour Defence was reduced to a active hard core of members. The NMM collapsed altogether. Finally, Hannington and other leaders of the NUWM opposed the 'third period' policy and for this reason, despite his being its best-known mass leader, he was excluded from the CP's inner leadership.

In his memoirs, 'Unemployed Struggles 1919-1936', the 'third period' barely warrants a mention. Ironically, the 'third period' was described by the Communists as being one of 'class against class'. In fact the real division that emerged was between the organisations and political institutions of a single working class. The reasons for the reluctance of the NUWM to embrace 'third period' tactical positions go deeper still. Opposition to the sectarianism and recriminations that characterised this period, ran deep in the CP, especially amongst its engineering and coal mining membership, many of who were leaders of the NUWM. This grouping, which included Wally Hannington, were able to delay full implementation of 'third period' policies right until the 12th CPGB Congress in December 1932. By then, the situation was so fluid that 'class against class' tactics were old hat. The experience of the NUWM was critical in bringing the CPGB out of the 'third period' dead end.

It is now accepted by a new generation of historians that the 'third period', used to stigmatise communists for generations, actually existed for a very short period and cannot be considered the whole story. In Britain, with its tradition of keeping division within the family and resolving problems by means other than splitting, the third period policies had no chance of success. Not that they deserved a chance. Hannington could see that they were a dead end and, within the constraints of criticism allowed by a centralist 'democratic' party, gave voice to his doubts. In the same way that communists are stigmatised for the 'third period' they are often praised for the unifying and anti-fascist role that they played from the mid thirties onwards based on policies adopted at the Seventh World Congress of the Communist International.

What historians often miss is the continuity of the dramatis personae that opposed the policies of the third period as they were unravelled and reformulated into the popular front of the mid thirties. In the case of France, Thorez openly and expressly opposed Comintern policy and achieved its change. That led to Europe's First Popular Front government. According to Carr in his book 'Twilight of Comintern', one of the British leaders who spoke against the 'third period' policy whilst in Moscow, was Hannington. Most importantly of all, he may have actively opposed or, at least, certainly never encouraged the calls made within the NUWM to embrace a more formal relationship with the CP. This call came closest to realisation at the third NUWM conference, held in Coventry in 1923. It was voted down by 55 to 52. Hannington knew that such a move would be the death of the NUWM. It would have done the CP no good either, simply locking it into a solar system of like-minded organisations, thus excluding the great mass of workers.

The damage wrought by the 'third period' schism had been done and lingered for many years. Those who had been called 'social-fascist' got their revenge during the Cold War when communists were barred from union election and office, often by those they had denigrated in the late 20s. There is a thread, best dealt with by one of the growing body of serious counter factual historians, which needs looking at. This is whether the NUWM and TUC could ever have enjoyed a formal relationship given the division into Second (pro social-democratic) and Third (pro communist) Internationals after the Russian Revolution of 1917.

With relations broken, both the TUC and the NUWM doubled their efforts to organise the unemployed. In reality, the TUC were starting from scratch and were unable to regain the ground that the NUWM had so painstakingly built up over seven years. Central to the failure of the TUC effort was the attempt to limit unemployed organisations by tying them to the trades' councils. This denied them the independent national voice that the NUWM had already developed. But the failure of the TUC was no compensation for the NUWM as they had effectively been cut off from the trade unions, and therefore any hope of real success. Much of the work of the NUWM in the 14 years following 1926 was aimed at achieving the type of acceptance in the mainstream labour movement that it had previously enjoyed. However it is important to recognise that, even had the TUC-trades councils' option been a success, it would still, because of the very nature of these councils, have kept the unemployed isolated from the employed, the very reverse of what was needed to create jobs.

Throughout the early 1920s, the trades councils actively campaigned for public works schemes to alleviate unemployment. Many of these campaigns, for instance in Liverpool, were directed by the NUWM. In this period neither the trades' councils nor the NUWM were allowed to affiliate to the TUC. A full year after severing relations with NUWM, the General Council began a study of the unemployed organisation set up by Bristol trades council, and formulated a scheme of its own. This scheme was aimed at the creation of Unemployed Associations (UAs) who would work directly under the trades' councils, to whom they had to submit all their business, and who had control of their accounts. The UAs had representation on the trade councils, but could only speak on the issue of unemployment. They were to have no general policy and their primary function lay 'in obtaining for unemployed persons as high a standard of living as possible, to deal with Government legislation and to provide educational, recreational and other facilities for its members'. Campaigning for job creation was not to be a priority.

The scheme came under heavy criticism at the 1928 Trade Union Congress. One delegate thought it was *"not our business"* to establish organisations *"in order to counteract the influence of the unemployed committee movement"*. A representative of the miners thought that the General Council's scheme would *"mean that you will have men and women paying dues to the trades council, and there will be no authority over them"*. The proposals were referred back to the General Council.

In the following year, those councils that had tried to inaugurate the scheme (as in Bradford) found themselves confronted by the hostility of the unions, making further operation virtually impossible. Often, the unions did not have enough trust or faith in the trades' councils' ability to organise the unemployed. Only six trades councils managed to operate the scheme with any success, despite growing support for the General Council's policy from the transport and railway unions.

Whilst the General Council floundered, the NUWM gained ground. The 1930 Hunger March, despite taking place at the height of Communist condemnation of Labour, gained widespread 'unofficial' support. The Labour Government fell in 1931 not least because of its failure to deal with unemployment, which must also have shaken much faith in the 'constitutional methods' of the General Council. Issues of great national import were being settled. In September 1931 Britain came off the Gold Standard. In order to find

NATIONAL UNEMPLOYED WORKERS' MOVEMENT.

MEMORANDUM
on the
DEVELOPMENT OF SOCIAL LIFE IN THE N. U. W. M.

In accordance with the decisions of our 8th National Conference at Manchester during Easter 1933, we have several times - in circulars - urged our branches to follow out the line of developing the social life in the N.U.W.M. to counteract the influence of the Social Service Centres among the unemployed. Several Branches have made good progress in this work, but there are still very many Branches that are not attempting to tackle the question at all. We are therefore issuing this Memorandum and urge that it be carefully considered in every Branch, and the necessary steps taken to carry out these lines of activity:

(1) HALLS. Each Branch should endeavour to get Branch premises with a suitable Hall attached that can be used for the social activities of the Branch. They should press the local authorities to provide them with such a Hall, and if they fail in this respect, they should approach any sympathetic authority in the locality who is able to place such a Hall at the disposal of the Branch, or they should even consider the question of hiring a Hall, providing the rent is within their means. The Branch could raise a special fund for getting the Hall, and probably the rent of same could be covered by the money raised through social activities.

It must be clearly understood that where the Branch has Branch premises or such a Hall at their disposal, there must be a Management Committee established, and that Committee must exercise the strictest control in respect to the management and conduct of the Hall. Strong action must be taken against any person or persons who seek to use the Hall in a manner likely to bring discredit on the Movement.

(2) CONCERTS, WHIST DRIVES & SOCIALS. The Branch should establish a Socials Committee that in its tasks makes arrangements for the organising of Concerts, Socials, Whist Drives, and other such social activities. These methods have been found over and over again to be very effective - if organised properly - in the raising of finance for the Movement. They also develop the socialability which we require between members and friends, and encourage new elements to come into our Movement. This work must not be relegated simply to the Womens' Committee. It must be regarded as the responsibility of the whole Branch.

(3) LIBRARIES. The Branch should endeavour to organise a small Lending Library. The books in such a Library should be principally of a technical character, dealing with the Working Class Movement, such as Industrial History books, books on Political Economy, on the Soviet Union, and general Working Class political books. Of course, some fiction books can also be included, but these are not so important. We want a Library utilised for the political development of the members of the Library. Ordinary fiction books can generally be obtained from any other Library. A small charge of say, 1d, should be made for books borrowed. Proper check of members must be kept and steps taken to see that books borrowed are returned in accordance with the rules governing the Library. The Branch could appeal to sympathisers to support us by giving books or buying books they borrow.

(4) STUDY CIRCLES AND CLASSES. It must be now regarded as an important task by every branch to organise Study Circles and Classes to train the membership on the questions affecting the Workers' Struggle.
A big weakness of our past work has been this insufficient attention to the need for Study on Working Class Problems.
Leadership cannot be separated from such studies and special Classes should be organised to develop discussion, to train speakers, and to bring forward new forces to strengthen the leadership and active members in all localities.
The books in Branch Libraries could serve to equip such Classes with material for Study.

a national voice the unemployed only had one place to go.

At the 1931 and 1932 congresses, marchers organised by the NUWM demanded action by the TUC on unemployment and many hostile scenes were recorded.

At its meeting in January 1932, the General Council decided it was time to re-establish the unemployed associations. They sent two representatives to a conference in Bristol in February 1932. Bristol was one of the few UAs that existed, based on the previous General Council scheme that had aroused so much union opposition. The General Council recognised two needs: an organisation to meet the social needs of the unemployed and a national voice to reach the Government. Yet in the major struggles of the decade, the NUWM had been to the fore and had built itself a reputation for legal representation of the unemployed, opposition to evictions, and an extensive network of sports and cultural organisations. As a national voice for the unemployed it may not have been the first point of call for the TUC, but it was really the only show in town. Only politics precluded the TUC from recognising this and finding a way to heal the rift. For the NUWM the rift had become a badge of honour.

The General Council sought to establish a federation of UAs under TUC control. The Bristol Association, the model for the scheme, rejected this move and no agreement was made. Despite this setback a federation was set up and the General Council issued a Model Constitution for the UAs under the auspices of the trades councils. This was presented to the 1932 Trades Councils Annual Conference, where the previous decisions of the opposition were reversed. Citrine pointed out that *"the Trades Councils were the only organisations available for such work"*. The Trades Union Congress held in September emphasised the need to oppose the NUWM after fierce rioting, which had broken out in Belfast, was blamed on the organisation. Against this backdrop the General Council Scheme was accepted.

But neither the UAs nor the trades' councils were immune from collaboration with the NUWM. The national hunger march of 1934 broke the back of the TUC campaign to win the unemployed away from the NUWM. Indeed, as the General Strike receded into memory, relations between the different organisations of labour changed. So too did policies. In some ways public relations between the NUWM and the Labour Party thawed more swiftly than between the NUWM and the TUC. For example, the Miners' Federation of Great Britain and many Labour MPs, including Clement Atlee, the Party Leader, who appeared on the platform at the final demonstration, supported the 1936 Hunger March. The General Council continued to circularise trades councils, advising them against helping hunger marches but to less and less avail. At the 1937 Trades Council Annual Conference, every speaker condemned the attitude of the General Council and General Council proposals to break all ties with the NUWM were voted down.

In 1938, the General Council was forced to admit that the majority of trades' councils on the route of the hunger march of that year approved of the action and gave material support. In 1939, the Annual Trades Council conference agreed a resolution stating that the moving force behind the defeat of the Government's latest unemployment benefits proposals, were the activities of the 'organisations of the unemployed' rather than the 'negotiation of the General Council'.

The reasons for the failure of the UAs lay in the concept rather than the practice. For many unions and the General Council, the UAs were 'feeding grounds for trade unions' and provided 'a useful auxiliary for the trade union movement'. One of the rules of the UAs stipulated that *"a member could rejoin the Unemployed Association after a period of employment only if he had been in a union"*. On the contrary, the NUWM saw one of its main aims as educating and organising, particularly amongst those youngsters who had never had a job, and to spread the ideas of trade unionism. In other words, they did not preclude those who had never been in a union but rather sought to draw them into the movement. For the TUC, the movement between union and unemployed organisations would take place only to the advantage of the unions.

A member of the Communist Party or any other organisation proscribed by the General Council could not be a member of an unemployed association after 1935, whereas the NUWM worked successfully with many organisations including those allied to the Liberal Party. It included Labour Party members even from its inner leadership and worked with activists drawn from the ranks of social reformers and churchmen. Because of these political restrictions, a number of trades' councils, including Deptford and Croydon had their recognition withdrawn for transgressions. The blacklisting of communists and the establishment of lists of proscribed organisations was as unlikely to work as the policies of a 'third period' CP for the simple reason that so many effective local organisers who would be available to build UAs for the TUC would be communists. Incidentally, the communists were proving to be among the best builders of the unions. Throughout the thirties, many a gold badge for best union recruiter was awarded by an unsuspecting TUC, to local activists who turned out to be members of the Communist Party.

Less than a quarter of the trades' councils expressed any interest in setting up UAs, many preferring to work with the established local NUWM branch. In 1936, in its report to congress, the TUC General Council complained that most of them preferred to leave the organisation of unemployed workers to non-union bodies. This was a poorly disguised swipe at the NUWM. In Scotland, the Scottish TUC General Council first tried to establish UAs in the winter of 1932, but over a year later, only two had been inaugurated. Glasgow and Edinburgh trades councils refused to set them up, insisting on working with the NUWM, and the local UA actually merged with its NUWM counterpart. This also happened in Oxford a year later. Despite ideological division it should have been obvious by 1935, that the answer for both sides was the formation of a new organisation out of a dissolution of the UAs and NUWM. This would have also provided the opportunity for bringing in other local, church and charity organisations that owed allegiance to neither of the two labour movement organisations.

Later that year the NUWM claimed 50,000 members as opposed to only 10,000 in the 'official' TUC organisation. At their peak in 1934, the UAs claimed 'over 120 branches' totalling some 22,000 members. Michael Foot says in his 'Autobiography of Nye Bevan' that *"the NUWM captured the field as the leading champion of the unemployed and showed no signs of being dislodged by the feeble and tardy efforts of the orthodox labour organisations"*.

It may be concluded that the General Council wished to create unemployed associations under its control and in its own image. They would be uncritical of TUC policy and only be allowed to speak on the issue of unemployment. But how could unemployment issues be divorced from other industrial and social policies? By creating organisations from the top downwards, rather than drawing in those that evolved and were tested in struggle - something being achieved by the NUWM in the face of General Council opposition - the TUC were actively forcing a division between the employed and the unemployed, the very thing they claimed they were attempting to bridge.

To join a UA, one had to have a union card and even then members could only discuss unemployment. This restriction did two things. It avoided contact with those millions who had never had a union or a job, and therefore ran aground on the reality that much of the strength of opposition to unemployment lay in the community. It was through social, sporting and agricultural activity in the shape of promoting allotments that many of these communities survived. Organisation purely on a trade union basis divided this base of support by excluding families or anybody without a 'union ticket'. It would also effectively restrict discussion and action on the issue of unemployment to the ex-trade unionist now without work. Yet the basic philosophy of trade unions is 'an injury to one is an injury to all' with individuals taking an equal share of responsibility for each other's welfare. There could never be, and can still not be today, an effective campaign to oppose unemployment based on dividing those with jobs from those without. It is unlikely that the unemployed, many of who were in the most desperate of straits, cared too much whether the organisation that sought to mobilise on their behalf was the NUWM or one led by the TUC. What mattered was getting things done.

During the worst years of unemployment between 1921-1924 and 1929-1934, the General Council failed to mobilise its constituent organisations to combat it or to ensure that the NUWM was drawn into the labour movement. Yet the TUC alone had the authority and leverage to create a new 'all in one' organisation for the unemployed. Alternatively, it could have used the changed circumstances of the 1930s, overshadowed by the growth of fascism, to bring the NUWM into the fold, but on more on TUC-friendly terms. It chose to do neither, opting instead to set up a further rival, to an organisation that had itself become a rival to the TUC. Michael Foot was right.

Can we lay the blame for the failure to forge this all-important unity exclusively at the feet of either the General Council or the NUWM? What do we gain by apportioning blame? Very little. For that reason it has been most important to understand the deep seated reasons why division arose and, more importantly, why it was sustained. History, even of the most partisan kind, is devalued by apportioning blame unless it is accompanied by an attempt to draw lessons. Yet, whilst disunity prevailed, the suffering of the unemployed was greater than it would have been, had unity been achieved.

Initially, both organisations were prepared to work together. Indeed the NUWM was prepared to be almost subservient to the policies of the General Council, an opportunity which that body rejected, seeing in the NUWM, as it had with the earlier shop stewards' movement, a parallel organisation in danger of bypassing the official one. Rather than drawing the NUWM in and developing it as an extension of the strength and organisation of the labour movement, it sought to rival it. After the General Strike came the 'black circulars', extending the exclusion of communists from the unions and the 'class against class' policy adopted at the sixth Congress of the Communist International, held in 1928. Although it was lukewarm in embracing this policy in private, the NUWM subscribed to it in public. This disastrously resulted in it aiming its core criticism at the supposed 'sell-out Labour bureaucrats' in equal measure to those who it claimed caused unemployment. It is impossible not to suggest that when the potential existed for united action, or even the creation of a new single organisation of the unemployed, each organisation put dogma before service. The relationship was to plumb new depths when, at the 1929 general election, two NUWM leaders, Geddes and Hannington stood against the official, trade union backed, Labour Party candidates in Greenock and Wallsend respectively.

The relationship of the CPGB to the NUWM has exercised historians for a number of generations and is likely to continue to do so. The relationship was certainly not a straight transmission belt of instructions, despite *'Hannington being released from other CPGB activities to concentrate on NUWM work'*. It is true that before 1936, aspects of CPGB policy towards the NUWM were discussed and often decided in Moscow, headquarters of the Communist International and Profintern (Red International of Labour Unions). Hannington was elected to the Presidium of the Profintern in 1930, where decisions were taken to launch international days of action against unemployment throughout Europe. But Hannington was no ordinary 'yes' man, being removed from CP leadership positions on a number of occasions because of differences over policy. At the 1929 CP Congress, he even gained the rare accolade of standing for and being elected to the party central committee against its own recommended list. Arthur Horner, CP member, a leader of the unemployed and future General Secretary of the Miners' Federation of Great Britain, was such another. These men tended to speak about things as they saw them, regardless of the official policy of the organisations that either employed them or of which they were members. Horner, for example, caused a storm when, at the height of the Cold War, and as leader of the National Union of Mineworkers, he spoke publicly in favour of French miners, striking against the USA-inspired Marshall Plan. These men were certainly not ideological robots.

In 1930 Hannington, aided by Syd Elias, was responsible for rebuffing a CPGB attempt to steer the NUWM away from individual casework among the unemployed denied benefits towards a more confrontational role. He was removed from the central committee in November 1932, accused of (in CP speak) excessive "legalism". Some of the best known leaders of the NUWM, including Fred Copeman, who fought as a battalion commander in the International Brigades in Spain, and Joe Jacobs of London's East End, were later expelled from the Party for adhering to policies on organising the unemployed, that were not in favour at party headquarters in King Street. This is not to say that anyone who opposed King Street was automatically right. What it proves is that there was a much more complex interrelationship between member and party than historians have often been able to admit.

They were Communists; brave and committed men and women too. Each faced imprisonment, sometimes forced into backbreaking labour or enduring the stress of solitary confinement. Even though their families suffered they remained unmoved. Their sole commitment was to the unemployed and no historian has been able to prove otherwise or demonstrate that they in any way suppressed the interests of those unfortunate people for purely party political gain.

Such characters were denigrated for their political beliefs. Yet they were a breed whose political beliefs were shaped before the CP or NUWM were formed. They gave allegiance to that party only insofar as they thought it represented their best hope in the struggle against capitalism. When it allowed dogma to hold sway they appear to have been adept at retaining their Party card while keeping their integrity intact. For a period between 1928 and 1932, the NUWM was the only CP-influenced organisation with any mass following or impact and it was their experience within this movement that helped the CP leaders pull their party back from its disastrous 'third period' course. Leaders like Hannington - steeped in labour movement traditions of discipline and unity, were uncomfortable with the CP policy of attacking Labour leaders even more vehemently than they did capitalists. Along with others from an engineering background such as Claude Berridge, he was rooted in the large engineering factories and workers' movement of West London, and sought first to deflect the negative effects, and then unravel the legacy of 'third period' sectarianism. In this way, the NUWM acted as a sort of back door for realism and pragmatism in the CP and it was precisely this approach that brought the Party such success during the latter 1930s and the war years.

After 1926, the NUWM overreacted and widened the divisions already created between them by the General Council. There followed a period of intense hostility with the General Council seeking to sabotage the NUWM's activities like the national hunger marches, cutting off much of the support that could have empowered the NUWM and thus the unemployed. Perhaps the greatest failure of the two bodies becomes evident when we ask the question 'was unity ever possible?' The answer to this must be 'Yes'. Each organisation tended to judge the other by its leaders, exchanging accusations of being 'reformist' or 'communist'. Failure to recognise common interests denies the basic tenets of trade unionism; that the interest of the members come first and the leaders act on the policy determined by those members. At all times, between 1921-39, the unified aim of the employed and the unemployed to end unemployment should have been of prime importance to the labour movement and should have been the starting point and basis of its activity, not the line of demarcation. The failure of the NUWM to consistently play a TUC-centred role was an inevitable outcome of the schism that developed, Europe-wide, in post-Russian Revolution labour movements.

A failure to put people and common policies first and labels second meant that unemployment and division continued and that people's needs were neglected and remained unfulfilled. The tragedy lay in the fact that at best the NUWM could only influence Government policy on levels of benefits and work schemes. It led activity, the extent of which has never been matched. This activity meant real sacrifice by thousands on behalf of their fellow unemployed. And even then it was not enough. Why? Because the answer to unemployment lay with the employers who were only influenced by the organisation of those they employed: unionised workers. Failure in unity resulted in failure to effect the real change that the NUWM had worked so hard for. The breakdown of relations between organised and unorganised labour found the NUWM forced to the margins, with the TUC attempting to establish rival organisations. To its credit, the NUWM never seriously tried to recruit unionised workers, away from unions and into active NUWM membership as a means of showing solidarity with the unemployed. Many employed workers did join as individuals, providing much needed finance and experience. But if the NUWM had taken such a formal step, it is unlikely that they would have recovered, for even their labour movement friends would have deserted them and they were entering a period when they would need every friend they could get.

It was during the 'Hungry Thirties' that the organisation faced its greatest challenge.

The NUWM In the Hungry Thirties

> "If you cannot solve a problem the natural thing to do is forget it; and this is what capitalism tried to do with the unemployed."
>
> Aneurin Bevan reviewing W Hannington's book 'Unemployed Struggles 1919-36' in 'Labour Monthly' December 1936

In the 1930s, the NUWM embarked on a struggle against almost insurmountable odds. Continuous demonstrations, marches and deputations show unrivalled levels of working class activity against unemployment, even compared with the time of the General Strike. They seem more akin to the days of the Chartists when thousands mobilised not just for days, but also over many years. The hunger marches involved unprecedented organisation and co-ordination. The first march had taken place in 1922. Two thousand South Wales miners had marched on London in 1927. But as a weapon to influence government policy, the marchers came into their own in the 1930s. Large, nationwide marches to London, including separate women's contingents, took place in 1932, 1934 and 1936, and there were more marches in Lancashire, Wales and Scotland. The 1932 march brought together as many as 18 separate contingents gathered from all areas of the country.

It also added a new formalised dimension to its activities. Spurred on, in part, by competition from other unemployed organisations, the NUWM reinforced its work of individual representation. Though this work never coexisted comfortably with its revolutionary ambitions, it appears to have been carried out most effectively, doubling the number of successful claims compared with those where an individual represented himself. It was in 1930 that the NUWM secured recognition by the National Insurance Umpire as an association of the unemployed, enjoying the same rights to represent individuals as that already given to trade unions. The individuals requiring help had to belong, which drove up membership figures but probably also increased membership turnover. As an organisation then spurned by the official Labour movement, and regularly appearing in newspaper headlines threatening red terror, the odds were heavily stacked against the NUWM actually achieving government authorisation to represent the unemployed. Having secured such recognition they were able to use it both effectively and well.

The 1930s tested the strategy of the NUWM but extended it too. First came the struggle against unemployment followed by the campaigns against the threat of war and fascism. From Spain onwards, these strands, anti-war, anti-unemployment and individual representation were conjoined. The link was accepted far beyond the ranks of the NUWM, but the nature of the challenge raised the stakes facing the organisation even further. Whereas in the 1920s, the workers' movement was concerned that the unemployed would be used as strikebreakers and looked to the NUWM to turn the unemployed away from such a path, by the 1930s, the concern was that the unemployed would turn to fascism.

In May 1929, the Labour Party was victorious in the General Election. For many, this second Labour government gave hope that what was later known as the 'Hungry Thirties' could be avoided.

Unemployment and the treatment of the unemployed were the main issues. In an interview on the eve of the Government's formation, Prime Minister-elect, Ramsey MacDonald had said: "In our first session we shall deal with unemployment and will bring relief and hope to the workers of this land". There was some administrative easing of the conditions of benefit payment, and the period of transitional payment was extended. Yet, by the autumn of 1929, cases of disallowance of benefit by insurance officers exceeded 308,000 as compared with 219,000 during the same period of the previous year. The imposition of 'test' and 'task' work as a condition for the receipt of poor law relief, long detested and which many Labour local authorities had refused to operate, was maintained. Indeed, the Ministry of Health, headed by Arthur Greenwood, rebuked Boards of Guardians who were not imposing any 'task' on relief recipients. The closed hand of Chancellor Snowden could be felt in every Government department.

A sensation was caused when building of the giant Cunarder cruise ship was halted in December 1931, throwing thousands of men out of work on Christmas Eve. It was a huge dent to the pride of the Cunard Company and the British ship-building industry, the importance of which should not be underestimated. The shift from black to red in the balance of payments in 1932 was largely a result of under-performance in invisible exports such as receipts from shipping and overseas investment. Exports had fallen 38 per cent whilst imports remained static. To counteract this, the newly elected National Government imposed a 10 per cent tariff on all imports from February 1932 except for items such as wheat, meat and wood pulp. In exchange for allowing these items to go untouched, countries had to buy British goods in return. Most items such as tea, sugar and cocoa faced a ten per cent tariff. Others such as cars and artificial fibres faced a McKenna duty of 33 per cent. For those countries that retaliated, the government took special powers to levy tariffs of up to 100 per cent, though these were never actually used. In this way it was able to force exports through the protective barriers of smaller countries. Tariffs were an offensive not defensive measure. But the retaliation of larger countries such as France and Germany particularly on the question of coal, or other large importers of British goods such as Poland, offset the effect of such measures. Even minor increases in the export of cotton to China and Hong Kong reflected more the boycott of Japanese goods. If anything, tariffs and depreciation only checked the growth of imports. They had little effect on raising the volume of exports in sectors such as machine manufacture. Here, depreciation had little effect because competitors had a greater rate of investment and higher level of technique and technology. Britain was moved in the direction of open protection.

Historically, countries such as Germany and the USA had effectively adopted protection when they were building up their industry. In the case of Britain it was being resorted to at a time of retrenchment. Chancellor Chamberlain advocated it as a way of encouraging companies to make good the investment gap in technology and technique. In fact it did much to encourage the formation of giant companies, but without the necessary improvements in productivity. It also encouraged foreign investment, with companies such as Ford and Citroen buying British factories as a means of evading import tariffs. It was inevitable that the extent of British industrial activity far outweighed the size of her domestic market. As such, pressure grew to extend the tariff walls to surround the Empire. But each of the main countries that made up direct colonies and dominions: India, Australia, New Zealand, South Africa and Canada for example, were building up their own industry. The attempt to enforce Empire preference on an Empire where the price of raw materials had collapsed was similar in effect to turning up the temperature on a pressure cooker. Each responded to attempts to enforce a right of passage for British goods with the imposition of their own tariffs and levies. Some even repudiated repayment of interest on loans to the mother country. Never again within the structures of Empire and "empire economic unity" would Britain enjoy exclusive sway as a producer of manufactures. Where she had faced competition from the likes of America and Germany in the run up to 1914, she was now being challenged in her own back yard. Canada began in this period to export cars to Britain. Those seeking outlets for their manufactured goods began to look outside the confines of the Empire. In a world filled with surplus commodities in search of markets, this increasingly meant the USA.

The depreciation of sterling was not successful because it was based on the premise that, when Britain removed herself from the Gold Standard, others would stay. But taking Britain out was like removing today's Germany from the Single Currency. As a result of Britain's withdrawal, others followed and the effects of depreciation were not great.

By the time the Wall Street crash of October 1929 had had its effect, the unemployment problem dominated all others. Richard Croucher quotes Sydney Pollard as estimating that, at this all-time low, half the British workforce was affected by unemployment

In June 1929, there had been 1,169,000 out of work. This figure had risen to 1,770,000 by May of 1930 and, by the end of that year, over 2,300,000 were unemployed. Even greater numbers were on short time working. See Tables 23 and 24.

Table 23 Extent of short time working in certain industries in October 1931

	Proportion of all employed working short time	Average hours lost during week by those working short time
Tobacco	49.3	8.5
Tailoring	41.0	12.0
Shirt and Blouse Trades	35.7	10.4
Bleaching and Blouse	35.6	14.9
Cutlery and Tool Trades	29.3	15.4
Pottery	27.1	15.5
Boots and Shoes	26.1	9.7
Steel Manufacture	24.9	15.3
Quarrying	21.4	10.3
Non-Ferrous Metal Manufacture	21.4	10.7
Engineering	20.9	10.5
Woollen and Worsted	20.5	11.7
Light Castings	19.7	9.6
Dressmaking	19.2	11.5
Gold, Jewellery, etc	19.1	13.1
Papermaking	18.4	8.2
Silk and Artificial Silk	16.3	17.8
Brewing and Bottling	16.3	9.2

Source: GDH Cole and MI Cole The Condition of Britain (LBC Gollanz 1937)

The failure of the Labour Government to implement even a minimum programme of economic reconstruction and development led to divisions and discontent not only within the labour movement but also within the Cabinet itself.

Table 24 Economic status of the occupied population of Great Britain in 1931 (000's omitted)

	Males	Females	Total	Per cent total
Managerial	1,029	152	1,180	5.5
Working on own account	922	351	1,273	6.0
Clerical, commercial, and professional	2,207	1,491	3,698	17.3
Agriculture and fishing (operative)	892	44	936	4.4
Other manual workers (including armed forces)	8,035	3,678	11,713	54.9
Unemployed	1,968	557	2,525	11.8
	15,053	6,273	21,326*	–

Source: GDH Cole and MI Cole *The Condition of Britain* (LBC Gollanz 1937)
* This total includes those serving in the armed forces abroad and those away on board ship at the time of the Census.

At the Labour Party's Brighton Conference in 1929, a critical debate took place on the treatment of the unemployed. A motion referring back a paragraph in the Parliamentary Report stating that the Ministry of Labour had not yet had an opportunity to deal with unemployed grievances was lost by a narrow margin of 100,000 on a card vote; 1,100,000 were in favour of the motion, a clear indication that opinion was divided and frustrations were building up.

The third national hunger march, this time against a Labour Government, converged on London in time for May Day. One of the banners declared, 'underfed, under-clad, under the Labour Government.' This hunger march is notable because it included, for the first time, a contingent of women drawn from Lancashire and Yorkshire who had been employed in the textile industry.

In December 1930, the Government appointed a Royal Commission on Unemployment. An interim report of the Commission issued in the following summer formed the basis of an Anomalies Bill that sought to close much-criticised gaps and disparities in standards of support for the unemployed. Becoming law in August 1931, the Anomalies Bill was to greatly discredit the Labour Government, for the discrimination that it introduced against unemployed married women, and for its attempts to roll back the benefit conditions previously enjoyed by casual and seasonal workers. This Act was to play a major part in the downfall of the Government in August 1931. A Special Economy Committee, formed at the same time as the Royal Commission also reported in July 1931, recommended a ten per cent cut in all unemployed benefits, as well as wage cuts for civil servants, teachers and the police. It also recommended reductions in health services and general child and maternity welfare expenditure, totalling some £96,000,000. This was the price to be paid for seeking to sustain the Gold Standard well past its sell-by date.

At the end of July 1931, when the Special Economy Report was issued, the number of registered unemployed stood at 2,713,350.

According to a lead article in the Daily Herald on 12 August 1931, Snowden, the Chancellor of the Exchequer, said *"I warn the nation with ever increasing urgency of the need for real 'national' economy"*, and, *"it can be taken for granted that the Labour Government will not shirk its responsibility"*. Widespread unrest and nationwide protests greeted the threatened economy measures and divisions within the Cabinet grew more pronounced, leading initially to a split that was followed by the resignation of the Government.

Immediately following the formation of the Labour Government, the NUWM had published an Unemployed Charter that contained 12 points.

1. Raise the benefit scales of the unemployed.
2. Remove the 'Not Genuinely Seeking Work' (NGSW) Clause.
3. Restore to benefit all unemployed persons who were disqualified under the previous Government's administration.
4. Make benefit continuous during unemployment.
5. Abolish the six days' waiting period; benefit to operate from first day of signing.
6. Introduce national plan of work schemes at trade union rates.
7. Abolish all test and task work under the Boards of Guardians.
8. Guarantee full trade union conditions for all unemployed transferred under the industrial transference scheme.
9. Give the lead for a general shorter working day without wage reductions, beginning with the mining industry and Government establishments.
10. Introduce a system of pensions for all workers over the age of 60.
11. Raise the school leaving age to 16 with Government maintenance grants.
12. Repeal the Guardian's Default Act and establish a national uniform scale of relief.

The unemployed movement conducted a national campaign around these demands and on Sunday, 31st July 1929, demonstrations took place in support of the Charter. Delegates were refused permission to talk to Margaret Bondfield, Minister of Labour. In the House of Commons, Bondfield, in answer to a questioning backbencher, refused to agree the removal of the 'Not Genuinely Seeking Work' Clause, going only so far as to propose additional machinery for the examination of claimants in the form of Boards of Assessors. These boards were established in November 1929 and were disliked by the unemployed from the beginning. According to Hannington, "*It was not new committees of enquiry that were needed but the complete abolition of the clauses that were robbing thousands of unemployed of their benefits every week.*"

The NUWM led a nationwide campaign for a boycott of these assessors. The struggle was particularly intense in Lancashire and Yorkshire and there were violent clashes outside labour exchanges all over the country. In Yorkshire an organised mass refusal of the unemployed to appear before the boards was very successful. According to Hannington, other districts followed this lead and there developed, in his words, "*an interesting contest with the Ministry of Labour.*"

The managers of the labour exchanges ruled that all claimants who refused to appear before the boards would be automatically disqualified from benefit and would forfeit their right to appeal. The issue of the legal powers of the boards of assessors was thus brought into dispute. Pressure from the unemployed meant that the chief insurance officer was compelled to rule that refusal to appear before the boards would not lead to automatic disqualification or loss of right to appeal. This was, in effect, the end of the boards of assessors. Hannington was making no idle boast when he claimed, "*our agitation had the effect of considerably modifying the administration of the boards, and, when the new Unemployment Insurance Act came into operation in April 1930, the machinery was scrapped.*"

The opening of Parliament on September 8 1931, dominated by the National Government, formed the opening page of a chapter that led to the sharpest social conflict of the inter-war years. It was in this period that the Government sought to cut the benefits of the unemployed and wages of public service workers by ten per cent and introduce sweeping cuts in social and local government spending. These cuts were those inherited from the previous Labour administration. In many ways, the defection of MacDonald, Snowden and Jimmy Thomas from Labour, allowed a realignment in the guise of a National Government, comprising those committed to the cuts. A means test was introduced that dealt in families instead of individuals. Hence the savings and earnings of a grandparent were set against the benefit needs of an unemployed son or granddaughter. It immediately affected one million out of three millions unemployed. The means test made receipt of unemployment benefit reliant on the answers to a variety of especially intrusive questions.

The possibility of a claimant being able to manage without assistance was examined. Questions were asked. Was anyone in the household receiving wages or other income? Was anyone receiving a pension? What sorts of assets were there in the home? Was there any other member of the family on relief or dole?

It is estimated that through the use of the means test, the unemployed were deprived of nearly £30,000,000 a year. Within a short time, hundreds of thousands had been disqualified from claiming benefits and were driven into destitution. In its first year of operation, half of all those coming within its scope were either granted benefits below the standard rate or else were refused it altogether. The numbers on poor relief rose sharply. It was intensely disliked by the unemployed both for the hardship and the loss of dignity it caused, and fostered a central campaign by the NUWM that is perhaps best recorded by the petition sent to Parliament in 1932.

In the first days of the struggle against the 1931 cuts, the NUWM was involved alongside teachers, civil servants and other public employees. This period, which started at the beginning of September 1931, lasted only until the second election in late October of the same year. The second period, in which the unemployed fought on alone, followed the implementation of the means test on 12th November 1931 and reached its height in the autumn and winter of 1932. From the outset, the meetings and demonstrations that were held all over the country were larger and more determined than any actions since the General Strike.

September opened with a march of unemployed Welsh miners to the Trade Union Congress in Bristol. When Secretary Citrine ruled against the attendance of a delegation from the marchers, a battle with the police took place outside.

In London on 11th October, following separate demonstrations by teachers and civil servants, they were joined by postal workers, and the unemployed to form a protest against the cuts that involved 100,000 people.

According to Alan Hutt, "the story of the weeks from the end of September to the end of October reads like a series of war communiqués".

From Scotland's industrial centres, to the mining valleys of Wales, came repeated news of defiance of the Public Assistance Committees and of clashes with the police. In London, demonstrations through Whitehall on 29th September and 6th October brought such violent clashes that later in October the police set up barricades to keep demonstrators away from Whitehall. In Lancashire, fire hoses were used to quell 'disturbances'.

After the General Election in October, the campaign against the cutbacks entered its second phase. The cut in teachers' and civil servants' pay was restored leaving the unemployed movement to fight on against the means test. Though many employed workers did participate in the larger actions of the unemployed, their organisations were not mobilised alongside them in the fight against the means test. Cases like the call of the anthracite district of the South Wales Miners' Federation for a one-day strike of protest against the means test were few. At this time, the General Council of the TUC was preoccupied with the 'harmful' activities of the NUWM and in January 1932, at the height of the struggle against the means test, it recommended trades councils to form local unemployed associations under their own auspices. However in Bristol, the trades' council refused to participate in the General Council plan and, indeed, worked alongside the NUWM against the means test. Bristol led the way for many trades' councils, beginning a trend of unified action.

From November 1931 to February 1932, the story of the autumn was repeated. Less in number but wider in scope, the campaign drew in the unemployed of the North East, Yorkshire and Merseyside, and these areas became scenes of major struggle. In a number of places the Public Assistance Committees were forced to modify the operation of the means test; in others, winter relief was secured.

With the approach of spring, the movement began to scale new heights. In Birmingham, over 40,000 signatures calling for the abolition of the means test were collected and on Newcastle Town Moor, a demonstration against this test was attended by over 100,000.

All these actions were either led or brought into focus by the NUWM that had now built up local strength and enthusiasm to a point where it could launch its long awaited national campaign. Many of the twelve hundred delegates who attended an NUWM conference at the end of May had walked for days to get to the venue. It was here that they endorsed plans for the campaign, which included the collection of signatures on a petition urging: the abolition of the means test; the repeal of the Anomalies Act; the restoration of the ten per cent cut in unemployment benefit; and the restoration of cuts in social services. The climax of the campaign was to be a national hunger march to London in the autumn.

The growing sympathy in the unions to the demands of the unemployed became apparent at the Trades Union Congress meeting at Newcastle in September 1932. After the usual regional march of the unemployed to the congress, there was a heated debate in which Secretary Citrine again accused the NUWM of being a communist organisation. Although his ruling barring

MASS MURDER

AN EXPOSURE OF THE MEANS TEST

By SID ELIAS
(National Chairman, N.U.W.M.)

PRICE ONE PENNY

Published by
THE NATIONAL UNEMPLOYED WORKERS' MOVEMENT
35 Great Russell Street, London, W.C.1
Printed by Watford Printers Limited, 58 Vicarage Road, Watford

the attendance of an NUWM speaker was upheld by 1,577,000 votes to 963,000, on this occasion, many people spoke up in the NUWM's favour. Sir Ben Turner pleaded that the marchers should be heard. Collick from the locomotive men said *"I would like a gesture to be made in this matter showing that Congress is going to get back to that real working class spirit that was its foundation"*. Brown, from the patternmakers, urged Congress to *"allow them to come and state their case and show them by the way we listen to them that we are with them heart and soul"*. A dispute over the way the votes of the miners had been cast could have meant a clear majority for the NUWM to be heard. But it was not to be.

Hardly had the Congress broken up than events in Birkenhead, on Merseyside, took a dramatic turn. In a three day battle in which the unemployed turned on unemployment authorities and police alike, over 100 people were hospitalised and 45 were arrested, including the local NUWM committee, several of whom subsequently received gaol sentences of up to six years. The Public Assistance Committee was forced to raise the scales of relief paid under the means test to full level of unemployment benefit, thus effectively making themselves redundant. These struggles, even when they became very violent, were focussed and efficient. The degree of organisation was high. So too was the level of discipline. Quite unlike the unemployment struggles of the 1880s that were also violent, those of the early thirties involved very little looting or damage to property.

Following the events at Birkenhead, tragedy struck in Belfast, where a battle to overturn the means test started on 10th October. By 14th October, there were 50 injured and 2 dead. Three thousand workers in the Belfast linen mills had struck in solidarity and the Belfast Trades Council had called its unions out on a general strike against police repression.

The Northern Ireland Government was forced to surrender, making substantial concessions to the unemployed. Maximum relief was now raised from 24 shillings to 32 shillings a week, while the scale for a man and his wife was raised from 8 shillings to 20 shillings a week.

Meanwhile, 2,500 hunger marches were advancing on London encouraged by the fact that the petition against the means test had secured over a million signatures. All sections of the national march were due to meet there on 27th October. The unemployed of London were themselves immersed in an intense struggle against the means test, which resulted in serious disorder at the opening of Parliament in October 18th. Provincial police were brought to London to supplement the metropolitan forces and thousands of special constables were mobilised to prepare for the arrival of the hunger marches. The press, as on previous occasions, *"were calling for drastic action by the Government... several... called upon the Government to prevent the marchers from entering London"*.

On the morning of 27th October the press announced on that all leave had been stopped for the Coldstream Guards stationed at Wellington Barracks, and that they were being held in readiness in case of trouble. As the contingents of hunger marchers entered Hyde Park at about 2.30 in the afternoon, the enthusiastic cheers of well over 100,000 people greeted them. Baton charges, by mounted police and those on foot, were powerless to break up the crowds and meetings and fighting spread from the park along Marble Arch and around Oxford Street.

As dusk fell, the clashes grew fiercer. Bugles were blown, announcing to all the demonstrators that the meetings had finished and gradually they retreated to the park to regroup in their separate contingents. The Scottish contingent headed by fife and drum band led the way towards the Fulham Road and Wandsworth workhouses where the marchers were to be accommodated. Turning toward the Bayswater Road many expected the clashes to resume but as Hannington later wrote *"the slightest panic at that moment would have surely led to a battle.... It was the steadiness and discipline which the marchers had developed on the road that saved the situation."* There was no further fighting that day.

Three days later, on the Sunday, 150,000 people, including many employed workers under their union banners, demonstrated in Trafalgar Square. Again violence flared and again police attempts to break up the meeting, (this time by driving motorbikes into the crowd), failed. According to Hannington this demonstration "was the biggest that had ever been seen in Trafalgar Square". The next big move was to be the presentation of the 'million signature' petition to Parliament on the evening of Tuesday 1st November.

John McGovern, MP, added fuel to the fire by lending official support to the various national newspapers calling for the arrest of the NUWM leaders and Hannington was later arrested and charged with 'attempting to cause disaffection among members of the Metropolitan Police, contrary to the Police Act of 1919'. Police cordons attempting to keep the demonstrators away from the Houses of Parliament extended as far as Kings Cross and Holborn. Battles took place throughout the East End between police and demonstrators attempting to pass police blockades and similar episodes took place as men from Battersea marched across the Thames.

The petition itself had been hidden in locked luggage compartments in

Charing Cross Station. A deputation under the leadership of Fred Copeman, famous for his part as an Invergordon mutineer, arrived at the station but were surrounded in the Strand and arrested. When the news of these arrests reached the ears of the demonstrators, they were infuriated. Fighting, perhaps the most vicious yet seen in London, spread along Whitehall, past the cenotaph, around Parliament and Westminster Bridge; it was at its fiercest around Charing Cross and Trafalgar Square and up the Haymarket into Piccadilly. It continued until midnight, but with the absence of the petition, the violence had little real object and petered out when police reinforcements were called in.

There was no further attempt to present the petition to Parliament. Hannington was imprisoned for three months and Syd Elias, the President of the NUWM, was tried 'as an agent of a foreign power', namely the Soviet Union, and gaoled for two years. Tom Mann, leader of the Great Dock Strike of 1889 and NUWM National Treasurer, along with Secretary Emrhys Llewellyn were both tried for 'inciting disturbances' and were imprisoned for two months. The year of 1932 was nearing its end and the means test was on the ropes.

The National Government had one last volley to fire in that year. In November, when unemployment stood at 2,800,000, the final report of the Royal Commission on Unemployment was published. The findings of the report formed the basis of the remodelling of the Unemployment Insurance and Unemployment Assistance Board Schemes and the new Act of 1934.

Whilst the Act was still in its early Bill stage, it was popularly dubbed the 'Slavery Bill'. The first section, dealing with Unemployment Insurance Benefit, lay down that the receipt of benefit would be conditional upon whether *"the claimant has attended a course of instruction if required by the Insurance Officer to do so"*. The second section, dealt with persons who had exhausted their statutory benefit. It made receipt of benefit from the Unemployed Assistance Boards dependent on the claimant being prepared to perform work under the Ministry of Labour, without wages, on reconditioning schemes, public work schemes, in labour camps and at industrial training centres.

It was very difficult to avoid work in these labour camps, as refusal to work meant withdrawal of benefit and removal to a workhouse to perform task work. Refusal to enter a workhouse could lead to prosecution under the Poor Law with possible imprisonment on a charge of wilful neglect of one's dependents. Those being trained under the industrial training schemes would have to work for three-month periods under the direction of local authorities *"at the rates of wages customary in the district"*. This formula was seen by many as an attack

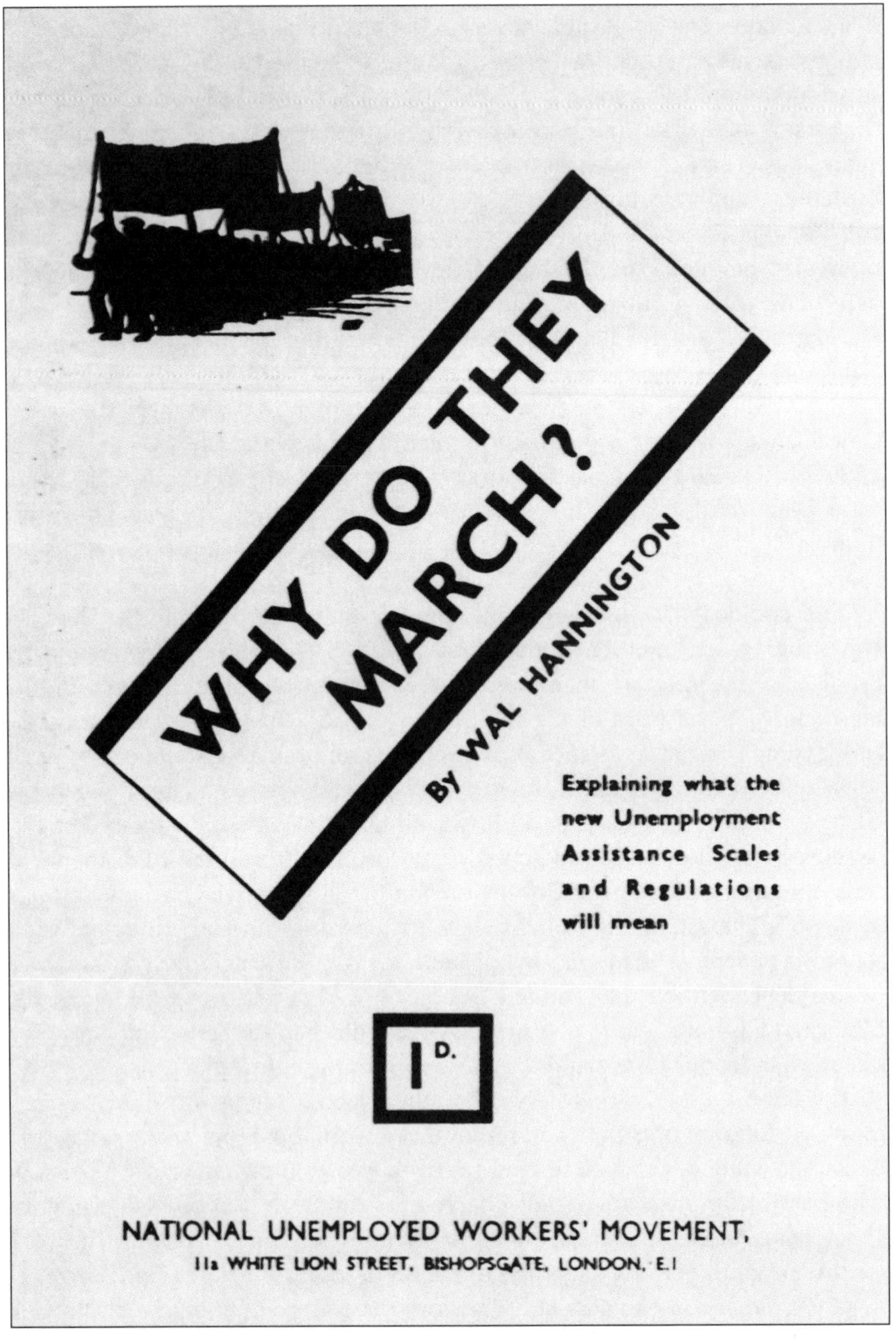
WHY DO THEY MARCH?
BY WAL HANNINGTON
Explaining what the new Unemployment Assistance Scales and Regulations will mean
1D.
NATIONAL UNEMPLOYED WORKERS' MOVEMENT,
11a WHITE LION STREET, BISHOPSGATE, LONDON, E.1

on trade union rates and thus on trade unions.

Along similar lines, the Bill was to refuse relief to a worker who lost his employment through a trade dispute. This was seen as an attempt to deter workers from striking. Between 1931 and 1933, the NUWM took 2,890 appeals of unemployed workers to the Umpire, the highest authority on the UABs, where they were successful in 1,020 cases. In January 1933, 17 months after the National Government took office, the number of registered unemployed reached the highest figures ever recorded in Britain – 2,903,000 – and if the unregistered were added, this figure would reach over 3,500,000.

Throughout the year a campaign took place against the activities of the National Council of the Social Services, which had come into being after the hunger march and 'disorders' of 1932. The Prince of Wales spoke in favour of social service centres *"to save the unemployed from demoralisation"*. These were centres where the unemployed could organise games and other activities the authorities encouraged, like taking part in voluntary work schemes or sharing out old clothes. In its literature, the NUWM, expressed the view that those behind the schemes: mayors; magistrates; and clergymen were *'honest but misguided'*. They called on the unemployed to resist poverty and not *'learn to live with it'*. Writing in 'Labour Monthly' in 1938 Hannington states *"We were convinced that the big drive at that time for the development of social service centres arose from the fear which had been engendered by the struggles which had taken place in 1932 in Belfast and Birkenhead and in the hunger march"*. But the centres were, more importantly, a move to prepare the way for a system of unpaid labour amongst the unemployed.

In its 1934 report, the Ministry of Labour, commenting on the activities of the centres welcomed *"the activities of voluntary organisations on behalf of the unemployed having developed considerably during the year, under the auspices of the NCSS, which undertook at the Government's request the work of co-ordinating and stimulating this movement"*. To the NUWM, this was an admission that the NCSS, supervised by some nine government departments, intended to establish some unwelcome principles and values into the new Unemployment Act. They were right to suspect this. The voluntary work schemes of the social service centres did prove to be forerunners of labour camps and the industrial training schemes. Worst still, it was known that some of those involved in drawing up such proposals had visited and been impressed by similar schemes operating in Nazi Germany.

In January, preceding the new Unemployment Act by six months and amidst

131

the Parliamentary debate on the Bill a national hunger march brought together even more support than that against the means test in 1932.

The situation was looking more hopeful. While the TUC General Council repeated it's warning to local labour organisations to have nothing to do with the march, the response of trades councils, Labour Party locals and trade union branches was exceptionally wide. When, after five weeks the marchers reached London, they succeeded in making those in Government take the issue of unemployment much more seriously. Significantly, probably as a result of the widespread support in official Labour circles, this time there were no police attacks on the demonstrators. The CP was emerging from its self-imposed 'third period' exile. It was negotiating with the ILP to establish a new party. Together they had called a 'Congress of Action' that involved unions such as the engineers in a way unheard of since 1926. Jack Tanner, President of the engineers, was amongst the representatives and as part of a 'United Front' Committee worked with the NUWM to organise the march.

The Government's refusal to meet a deputation of the marchers aroused a storm of criticism in the House of Commons and in the press. The Archbishop of York, supported by ministers of religion and MPs, took this opportunity to demand the restoration of the cuts in unemployment benefit. Even the Chamber of Commerce urged the Government to organise public works schemes. Seventy Conservative backbenchers had supported an opposition motion increasing child dependants allowance by one shilling, causing great alarm in the Cabinet.

The march had set demands for the restoration of the cuts in motion. Liberals, the clergy, the co-operative conference (then meeting in Glasgow), and many national trade unions all began to pressurise the Government. At a Conservative banquet in Birmingham on 9th March, Neville Chamberlain, Chancellor of the Exchequer, admitted that he was being overwhelmed with letters urging the restoration of the cuts. He particularly complained of the letter written by the Archbishop of York to 'The Times', urging all christians to support the campaign to restore them. The weekend before the annual Budget was to be announced, the NUWM called for a national demonstration and that same week Chamberlain announced that the scales of benefit were to be restored to their 1931 level. This meant that all claimants would receive a ten per cent increase. Although it could not claim sole responsibility for reversing the Government's decision, there is no doubt that this restoration represented a very important achievement for the NUWM. To be more precise it was a significant achievement for an NUWM that had turned away from the divisive and name-calling approach of the turn of the decade to one that sought maximum unity towards a specific end.

Concurrently with the restoration of the cuts the government announced its intention to look into those specific parts of the country known commonly as the "distressed" areas. This was a tremendous boost to the NUWM, who had campaigned for 14 years for such an investigation.

The findings of the commissioners were a shock. See Table 25. For example, the report of Captain Euan Wallace of Durham and Tyneside, showed that there were 147,940 persons unemployed in that area, of which 63,046 had been out of work for two years or more; 40,729 for more than three years and 9,246 for more than five years. In the Bishop Auckland area he reviewed, unemployment was 50.4 per cent of the insured population; in Jarrow it was 56.8 per cent.

Table 25 The Duration of Continuous Unemployment Periods for which unemployed workers had been continuously without work in July 1936

	Nos in thousands	Per cent of total
Less than 6 weeks	638	45.2
6 weeks - 3 months	149	10.7
3 months - 6 months	131	9.3
6 months - 9 months	89	6.3
9 months to 1 year	65	23.9
Total	1,409	100

Source: GDH Cole and MI Cole The Condition of Britain (LBC Gollanz 1937)
This table refers only to workers aged from 16 to 64 who were applying for benefits or allowances. It thus excludes those who had lost their claim to help except through the Public Assistance Committees.

Sir Wyndham Portal reviewed the South Wales area. There the proportion of unemployment in the Western area was 28.6 per cent compared with an Eastern average of 44.5 per cent. In Blaina, Bryn Mawr, Merthyr Tydfil – all mining centres - unemployment was 71.4 per cent, 72.5 per cent and 67.6 per cent respectively. More than a third of the workers in South Wales had been unemployed for more than three years.

In order to understand why there was a deeper awareness and greater

TEL.: BISHOPSGATE 3994

NATIONAL UNEMPLOYED WORKERS' MOVEMENT
(NATIONAL ADMINISTRATIVE COUNCIL)

Official Organ:
UNEMPLOYED LEADER
ONE PENNY

National Headquarters:
11A WHITE LION STREET,
LONDON, E.1

Circular No.D.39   6th February, 1935.

To all Branches, District Councils
and Women's Sections.

SMASHING VICTORY FOR N.U.W.M. !
FOLLOW UP FOR COMPLETE ABOLITION OF THE ACT !

We have scored one of the greatest victories in the history of the British working class movement. The National Government, in face of the tremendous storm of working class demonstrations and mass action, led by the N.U.W.M., has been compelled to make a humiliating retreat to restore the cuts that were imposed under the new scales and to suspend the operation of Part II of the Unemployment Act.

This is what mass action has been able to do in a period of four weeks from the commencement of the operation of the new scheme. It is an emphatic answer to those tame reformist labour leaders who have constantly told the workers that they must wait till the next General Election before they can remedy their grievances. Our Movement has consistently fought against such a defeated line. Our persistent drive for militant agitation and particularly the way in which we have swung millions of our class into united front action during the past month has made this National Government, even with its enormous majority in the House of Commons, beat a hasty retreat.

This victory will give an extraordinary stimulus to the Movement everywhere throughout the country. It is the most outstanding proof that has yet been given of the correctness of the line of the N.U.W.M. - its line of mass struggle based upon the unity of the unemployed workers and the bringing in of the employed workers in support of this struggle. Now, more than ever, our whole energies must be directed towards the greatest demonstrations that have ever been seen on February 24th. We must bring out clearly before every worker, employed and unemployed, what mass action has done, and from this show what mass action can do.

The intention of the National Government is to limit their retreat to a number of modifying amendments to the Act. This is clear from the statement made by Mr. Oliver Stanley, the Minister of Labour, in the House of Commons. When he agreed to restore the cuts, he said: "I have little doubt that the Regulations of the new scheme are sound in principle and that a large part of the dissatisfaction and the grievances which have occurred are due to the rigidity inherent at the inception of a new and gigantic scheme of this kind." "I have little doubt a substantial part of the remaining complaint can be cured by amendment of the Regulations."

We have forced the suspension of the second part of the Act. Now we must go forward with all our forces for its complete withdrawal; for the abolition of the Means Test; for the abolition of the Slave Camps; but even as we go forward we must understand that just as we expect to develop the movement a hundredfold so we must develop its organised expression - the N.U.W.M. - a hundredfold.

DRAW THE LESSONS - BUILD THE MOVEMENT

In all our agitation we must point out clearly to the workers how this retreat of the Government has proved the correctness of the work of our Movement and justified the line of militant agitation. We must show how the

(Please turn over)

concern amongst the unemployed and the employed in 1934 than there had been previously, we need to consider the plight of the distressed areas.

Compelled by the great national march of January and February 1934 to take special steps with regard to these districts, the Minister of Labour announced on April 19th that the Government had decided to conduct enquiries into the problems experienced in the distressed areas. The reports from these enquiries, published in October 1934, formed the basis of the 'Depressed Areas Development and Improvement Bill' that became law on 13th December 1934. Under this Act, commissioners were appointed *"to initiate, organise, prosecute and assist measures designed for the economic development and social improvement of the depressed areas"*. Government thinking about intervention in the economy was beginning to change - albeit under duress.

The areas that roughly constituted distressed areas under the Act were – West Cumberland, Lanarkshire, Durham, Tyneside, South Wales and Monmouthshire, Dumbartonshire, Stirlingshire and Ayrshire. The total population covered by these areas was approximately 2,800,000 in England and Wales, and nearly 1,000,000 in Scotland. In September 1936, the total number of registered unemployed people in these special areas of England and Wales was 282,952 and, in Scotland, over 80,000.

According to Hannington who made a study of these depressed areas, *"a very large proportion of these workers have been unemployed for more than five years, in some cases there has been continuous unemployment for ten years"*. See Table 26.

Table 26 Unemployment by areas, July 1936

	Nos unemployed thousands	Per cent unemployed	under 25	25-45	45-60	over 60
London	156	6.5	19.0	40.7	30.7	9.6
S. Eastern	61	5.6	19.0	41.6	28.7	10.7
S. Western	76	7.8	15.7	42.5	30.0	11.8
Midlands	181	9.4	13.3	41.5	33.6	11.6
Great Britain and Northern Ireland	1,717	12.7	16.8	45.0	29.2	9.0
N. Eastern	362	16.6	15.3	45.9	29.7	9.1
N. Western	359	16.2	17.1	45.9	28.8	8.2
Scotland	268	18.0	20.2	47.8	24.8	7.2
Wales	188	28.5	15.7	46.4	30.0	7.9
N. Ireland	65	23.0				
Special Schemes (Banks and Insurance)	–	1.6				
Age Distribution of Occupied Population (GB 1931)			31.7	39.2		29.1

Men only, G.B. only. Age distribution of unemployed over 18. Per cent of total unemployed in areas.

Source: GDH Cole and MI Cole The Condition of Britain (LBC Gollanz 1937)

The commissioners had only £2 million at their disposal to develop the distressed areas. Many people had originally thought that the Act marked a turning point, expecting the Government would now act decisively on unemployment. The Labour opposition had voted against the Bill. Aneurin Bevan, representing the Ebbw Vale district, part of the South Wales distressed area said in the debate, "The whole thing is an idle and empty farce, never intended to do anything. The Government are mocking the distressed areas with a proposal of this kind". Another MP, JJ Lawson, said "The average person will think this Bill is really designed to do something effective, deep and widespread, but as a matter of fact, the real purpose... is to appoint commissioners who are to shoulder in these areas responsibilities which the Government has shelved".

Given the scale of the problem, the resources allocated to it speak volumes.

One of the most terrible aspects of the distressed areas was the way in which the lives of younger people were affected. An example of the way in which young men's health was undermined by conditions of unemployment, poverty and lack of nourishment is revealed in the British Army Council Report of 1935. It shows that out of 80,203 young men who offered themselves as recruits for the army, 54,639 were rejected because they were physically unsound. Only 25,564 passed the medical.

At the root of the problem was a lack of industry and mechanisms that could direct capital towards large-scale projects of infrastructure building and manufacturing. The commissioners were not allowed to deal specifically with questions of employment in the short or medium term, only the long-term, but even this was restricted as we shall see. When giving his second report, Commissioner Sir Malcolm Stewart noted that *"Relief work designed solely to give employment, but having no further objective, was not to be entertained by the Commissioners"*. Thus, the commissioners were hindered in their work by the constraints of a government that had already rejected the idea of providing relief employment. Each proposed scheme of public utility was to be endorsed *"to the extent to which the work, when completed, would lead to the permanent economic development of the area"*. This may sound laudable but was in fact a ploy used to avoid providing direct Government underwritten employment. The constraints on the commissioners are best illustrated by the case of the Severn Bridge Scheme that we will look at in some detail in due course.

For the NUWM it was clear that any employment was not to come from those capitalists who always wanted more from less, but that the Government must assume the responsibility for providing jobs. They had sound reasons for this view.

Their arguments were backed conclusively by a survey conducted by Sir Malcolm Stewart in 1934. Stewart states that when he first took up his labours as Special Commissioner, he approached the Federation of British Industries to ask for their assistance. The FBI was encouraged to circularise employers for suggestions as to how the special areas could be revived and whether they would assist in establishing new industry or a branch of their business in these districts. Sir Malcolm writes *"the completion and return of the questionnaire entailed no expense and involved a minimum of labour"*. Yet, in spite of this, out of a total of 5,829 employers who had been contacted, 4,066 ignored the correspondence. There were 1,763 replies, but only 64 provided useful ideas and favourable answers to the questions asked. Unqualified negative replies to all questions came from 1,313 and 386 gave qualified negative replies. Out of the 64 who answered favourably, only 38 were ready to offer concrete assistance in the establishment of new works in the special areas.

If the commissioners could not provide relief work and the 'captains of industry' would not lend their aid, this further increased pressure on the Government, who alone were in a position to provide employment. Alas! the Government itself had a far from praiseworthy record in this field.

With regard to the question of establishing industries there, several industrialists had complained to Commissioner Stewart of the 'inaccessibility of South Wales'. Since he had taken office, Stewart had urged the construction of a road bridge over the River Severn, in order to open up South Wales to heavy motor and tourist traffic and to provide an alternative route to the existing one that meant passing through Gloucester and Monmouthshire. The proposed bridge would save 50 miles for road traffic, provide several thousand jobs for at least three years and further 'open up' South Wales to commerce and trade.

The proposition was submitted to the Ministry of Transport, who agreed to offer local authorities a grant of 75 per cent towards the cost of the project, which was not to exceed £2,480,000. The Government referred the proposition to a Select Committee of the House of Commons where it was rejected. (At the time, it is estimated that the Government was saving some £30 million through the means test). Stewart then appealed for further discussion on the matter and for Parliament to debate the scheme as a 'measure of first-rate importance'. The Government again refused. At this time, the railway companies had a monopoly on transport moving between England and Wales through the Severn Tunnel and knew that they would lose heavily if a main road bridge was built.

Stewart said of the Severn Bridge scheme in his third report to Parliament, *"I have been assured by several leading industrialists in South Wales that they are wholeheartedly in favour of the scheme but, unfortunately, vested railway interests and some important coal owners maintain their opposition"*. Hannington wrote of this incident *"One thing stands out very plainly in respect of the work of the distressed areas commissioners in the last two years, namely that these commissioners can spend their time preparing reports... but the Government has no serious intention of really acting upon the proposals contained in these reports to the benefit of the unemployed"*. Herbert Shaw speaking at the Church Assembly Conference in November 1936 backed up Hannington's charge. He said that Commissioner Stewart *"had been hampered in his work at every stage by red tape and had never had a free hand"*. Though much criticism was levelled

The PROBLEM of the DISTRESSED AREAS

By Wal Hannington

PRICE ONE PENNY

Published by the
NATIONAL UNEMPLOYED WORKERS' MOVEMENT,
11a WHITE LION STREET, BISHOPSGATE, LONDON, E.1

against the commissioners, at the time, it is clear that the responsibility lay at the feet of the Government who had the final say in any major work undertaken in the special (distressed) areas.

Conditions for the unemployed could only grow worse. The birth rate in 1935 had fallen to 14.7 per thousand, compared with 22.4 per thousand in 1921. The diet of the average unemployed family, especially of the long-term unemployed, consisted chiefly of bread, margarine, tea, potatoes and rice. Quality foods like milk, eggs, butter, fish, were rarely eaten. The incidences of infant mortality were higher in the distressed areas than anywhere else in the country. In 1931, there were 43.5 per cent more infant deaths in the distressed areas than in the rest of the country. In 1932, it was 31 per cent; in 1933, 45 per cent; in 1934, 32 per cent and in 1935, 41 per cent.

Poor nutrition was partly responsible for the high rate of illness. The increase in the number of deaths resulting from serious illness in distressed areas was high. In the case of bronchitis, 38.2 per cent, and 52.5 per cent in the case of pneumonia. In the case of tuberculosis between 1931-35, the figure ranged from 19 per cent to 30.5 per cent. All these conditions are associated with and exacerbated by poverty, joblessness and poor housing.

Awareness of these conditions helps us to understand the desperation felt by so many unemployed, a desperation that motivated them to fight against the New Unemployment Act of 1934, the means test and the labour camps.

Having driven the Government to restore the ten per cent cuts in unemployment benefit, the NUWM now focussed its activity on the Unemployment Bill that had come into force in July. The 1934 Act made radical changes to the whole system of unemployment insurance and was in three parts:
1. the Unemployment Insurance Act, dealing with all unemployed claimants on statutory benefit;
2. an entirely new scheme for creating an Unemployment Assistance Board (UAB), to deal with all claimants who had exhausted their statutory benefit and all able-bodied persons in receipt of Poor Law relief; and
3. the appointment of an Unemployment Insurance Statutory Commission to enquire into the working of the Act to make recommendations every year as to changes in amounts of benefit or of contributions or in administration.

Only Part 1 of the Act came into operation on 26th July 1934, the date fixed for the operation of Part 2 being 7th January 1935. The Act lowered the age of entry to unemployment insurance from 16 to 14 years of age. Receipt of benefit was dependent on the claimant having paid 30 contributions in the two years preceding application. Having satisfied this regulation, the claimant could draw benefit for 26 weeks. At the end of this period, if still unemployed, the case could be reviewed and additional benefit was given for three days, for every five contributions paid in the five years since the first claim, less one day's benefit for every five days benefit received during those five years. The other regulations governing Part 1 of the Act were the same as those previously in force.

It was Part 2 of the Act that caused a storm against the Government in the winter of 1934. There were 1,250,000 persons on benefit who, on 7th January, would pass to the control of the Unemployment Assistance Boards [UAB]. The threat of labour camps also hung over those able-bodied then in receipt of poor law relief who were to come under the direction of the UABs in March 1935. Hannington says *"Detailed regulations governing the operation of Part 2 were not made known until December 1934 but we knew enough of the main principles of the scheme to describe it justly as the most severe attack ever launched against the unemployed"*.

By October, serious opposition was sweeping the country, demanding the withdrawal of the Act and the granting of increased winter relief for all unemployed. The unemployed particularly disliked and distrusted those provisions for compulsory training under the UAB in either residential or non-residential training centres. This meant possible removal from their towns and families, working under near military discipline and receiving only four shillings a week pocket money, while the rest of the family survived on the allowances provided by the UABs.

The NUWM saw this as a danger to the trade unionism with which they identified and likened the camps to those in Germany.

Their fears were substantiated when the newspaper 'The People' quoted Sir John Gilmour, the Home Secretary, as having described the proposed labour camps as 'concentration camps'. Hudson, Secretary to the Minister of Labour, speaking in South Wales on 27th September 1934 said *"The new Unemployment Act is the best Act of our generation, because it will provide discipline and instruction to the unemployed youth"*.

On 1st October 1934, the NUWM campaign started in earnest. One thousand unemployed marchers from Monmouthshire to Newport demanded increased scales of benefit and an end to the slave camps. In South Wales, the police using low-flying aeroplanes broke up a large demonstration. In

Bridgend, the demands of a deputation that the authorities refuse to implement Part 2 of the Act was only narrowly rejected. Marches in the Rhondda, Glasgow and Sheffield in the second week of October secured increases of two shillings a week from the Public Assistance Committees (PAC). Agitation for improved benefit scales continued in all the major industrial centres, with varying success.

The PACs often claimed that the relief was not low but that the average working-class housewife lacked knowledge of food values and therefore did not buy the type of food necessary to keep the family healthy. In answer to this, Dr J R Marrack, a Professor of the University of London, speaking at Ruskin College Oxford, on 9th October said *"No amount of education in food values will make it possible to feed a child on two shillings, or a family on three shillings a head per week. The best protection against disease is to be the child of well-to-do parents"*. Try clothing them on that money too!

On 8th, 9th and 10th December 1934, the ninth National Conference of the NUWM was held in Keir Hardie Hall in Derby. Realising the gravity of the situation, and anticipating a change in relations between the NUWM and the TUC, a decision was taken to approach the General Council of the TUC with a view to united action. In reply to a letter along these lines, Secretary Citrine wrote:

"Dear Sir
I am in receipt of your letter of the 13th December, forwarding the resolution of your conference held in Derby from the 8th to the 10th December.
   Acting under instructions, I have to inform you that I cannot in future reply to communications from your organisation."

Immediately following the conference, the new scales and regulations of Part 2 of the Act were made known. The whole country was shocked by the ferocity of the reductions that ranged from two shillings to nine shillings. The only increase came in the area of child benefit, the maximum rise being two shillings and six pence. The means test was to be used more stringently with the whole family being assessed. Each member was only to be allowed five shillings personal savings after which point the test would come into operation. All income over five shillings earned by a family with one or more in employment, had to be used to maintain dependents or unemployed family members. Failing this, no benefit would be paid. A rent allowance that the Government had previously hinted at was simply made part of the payments scale.

Following publication of the new rules, large marches took place in Glasgow, and Bradford and a march in Hull led to widespread clashes and violence. The Norwich City Council meeting, on 19th December, passed a resolution denouncing the new scales. The new rates were received with anguish in the first week of January 1935 with many disallowed from receiving benefit because of the means test. On 20th January, 60,000 employed and unemployed marched through the Rhondda Valley and strike action was being discussed in many pits following an 'action' meeting of the executive of the Miners' Union on the 5th January. On 21st January, 40,000 marched in Merthyr demanding that *"the Act be not amended, but ended!"* Two days later, 20,000 marched both in Glasgow and Pontypridd demanding the withdrawal of the Act. Not only did unions take part, thus disavowing the policy of the TUC General Council, but shopkeepers also joined the activities.

On 26th January, the Scottish National Council of the NUWM organised a hunger march of 3,000 workers to arrive in Glasgow in mid-March and the unemployed of London 'invaded' the House of Commons on Monday 28th January.

When the UAB regulations had been issued, the Government had declared that they were final and unalterable but in the face of widespread opposition, they began to backtrack.

However, certain concessions relaxing the operation of the means test went unheeded by the unemployed and activity was stepped up.

The Manchester Guardian estimated that no less than 300,000 workers marched in South Wales on 3rd February. The TUC, the Labour Party and the Co-operative Society then issued an 'Appeal to the Public Conscience', urging the Government to withdraw the Act. They were all in effect, falling in behind the NUWM. The second week of February saw demonstrations in Scotland, Lancashire, Nottingham and Derby, Cumberland, Cheshire, Yorkshire and the Midlands. Thirty thousand marched on Tyneside.

On 5th February, the National Government bowed before the storm. In the House of Commons, Mr Oliver Stanley, Minister for Labour, announced that the Part 2 scales and regulations were to be withdrawn, the old scales were to be re-introduced and the cuts made under the new Act restored and that this would happen within two weeks. The Government were forced to suspend their new scales for over a year, though the Act remained intact through to the general election in late 1935, and they were unable to put Part 2 of the Act into full operation until the autumn of 1937. In the meantime the unemployed were still able to obtain extra winter relief from the Public Assistance

Committees. The election again produced a National Government. But it would be many years before a government could again launch such an assault on the unemployed. A stunning victory, perhaps the greatest for the NUWM, had been achieved.

Given even the most dispassionate assessment of the NUWM's impact it is quite inconceivable how so many historians have been able to write them out of the history of this period. Imagine the Government of today being first of all stopped in its tracks and then put into reverse by a similar organisation. Visualise 300,000 men and women on the march in South Wales.

In 1936, the struggle against the National Government surged again with the announcement of new UAB scales of benefit. A new hunger march directed against the means test was planned for the autumn. In scale and scope, this march surpassed even that of 1934. It gathered veterans of all walks of life to help the unemployed. Richard Croucher's investigation has shown that *"there were two dozen councillors in the Welsh contingent alone"*. Initiated by the NUWM, it gained support from all sections of the labour movement in most localities. In London, for example, for the first time, the march reception committee was formed under the official auspices of the London Trades Council, technically the London representative of the TUC. When the 2,000 marchers, coming from as far north as Aberdeen, from the Clyde and the Tyne, from Lancashire and South Wales, arrived in Hyde Park on Sunday, 8th November, they were greeted by possibly the largest demonstration yet seen in London. Estimates of those taking part vary between 150 and 250 thousand.

The strength of feeling across the country forced the NUWM and TUC to unite. Clement Atlee, Leader of the Labour Party, Wal Hannington and Aneurin Bevan shared the same platform. In its annual report for 1936, the London Trades Council wrote "the most significant feature of the march was the support given by people of all classes, creeds and politics". Britain was changing: had changed. The breakdown of relations between the NUWM and the TUC took place in a decade in which the country was recovering from war. By the mid-1930s, the NUWM was allowed back into the family of Labour, if not into the TUC, in a country moving towards another war.

THE NEW REGULATIONS EXPLAINED

SPECIAL   ONE PENNY

CUTS IN BENEFIT

For Married Couples and Single Men

	New scale	Present U.A. scale	Trans. Benefit
Single Men	15/-	15/-	17/-

So Single men will suffer a cut of 2/- per week.

	New scale	Present U.A. scale	Trans. Benefit
A Widower	16/-	15/-	17/-

This means that widowers will suffer a cut of 1/- per week.

Below are set out the actual new scales which the U.A.B. proposes to make and a comparison made with the present payments under the Unemployment Assistance Payments.

From this scale it will be seen at a glance that small increases will be granted to:

(1) A female householder with no husband is increased from 14/- to 15/-.

(2) A female over 18 living in lodgings or as a boarder is increased from 14/- to 15/-.

(3) A female under 18 living in lodgings increased from 12/- to 15/-.

A male under 18 living in lodgings increased from 13/- to 15/-.

It has to be noted, however, that in those cases, the U.A.B. has got powers to decrease the allowance in particular cases, and those who have had experience of how the Boards use their discretion, will readily realise that they will do all in their power to keep the allowance as low as possible.

Transitional Benefit Abolished

But the big outstanding feature of the scales is the fact that since the Standstill Order of February, 1935, was introduced when the government was compelled to restore the cuts, all married couples and single men, have been paid according to the Transitional Benefit rate as this was higher than the Unemployment Assistance scale.

Now both these sections will suffer a cut in benefit as follows:

	New scale	Present U.A. scale	Trans. Benefit
Man and Wife	24/-	24/-	26/-

So they receive a cut of 2/- per week.

THE SCALE

The following table drawn up by the Unemployment Assistance Board sets out the existing assistance scales and those proposed in the New Regulations.

Members of a Household.	Existing U.A. Regulations	New Regulations
A—Applicant, a member of a household consisting of two or more persons:		
For the household and the householder's wife or husband	24s.	24s.
For the householder:		
Male, without wife	16s.	16s.
Female, without husband	14s.	15s.
For each member of the household to whom the foregoing rates do not apply:		
If aged 21 years or over:		
Male—First member	10s.	10s.
Subsequent member	8s.	
Female—First Member	8s.	9s.
Subsequent member	7s.	
If aged 18 years or over but less than 21 years		
Male	8s.	8s.
Female	7s.	
If aged 16 years or over but less than 18 years	6s.	6s.
If aged 14 years or over but less than 16 years	6s.	6s.
If aged 11 years or over but less than 14 years	4s. 6d.	4s. 6d.
If aged 8 years or over but less than 11 years	4s.	4s.
If aged 5 years or over but less than 8 years	3s. 6d.	3s. 6d.
If under the age of 5 years	3s.	3s.
Where the household consists of only one child in addition to not more than two adults, the amount allowed in respect of that child shall be not less than 4s.		No change
Where in any household there are more than five members, the total for that household shall be reduced by 1s. in respect of each member in excess of five.		Provision deleted.
Lodgers and Boarders:		
If aged 18 years or over:		
Male	15s.	15s. Subject to adjustment by way of increase or reduction to meet the circumstances of a particular case.
Female	14s.	
If under the age of 18:		
Male	13s.	
Female	12s.	

The Hungry Thirties And The Approach Of War

Until the beginning of the War in 1939, the NUWM continued the fight against the Unemployment Act and means testing, but this area of its struggle, which had now passed its high point, was increasingly entangled with questions of fascism and the threat of war. Fascism was a challenge for a number of reasons. It threatened the conscription of labour and sought to divide communities by turning worker against worker. Fascism abroad had resulted in the destruction of union and labour movements, key allies of the unemployed. The approach of war raised the threat of conscription of another kind. The growth of the war industry, although slow and hesitant, was not the kind of employment that the NUWM favoured. A number of important NUWM leaders suspected that rearmament was to be directed against the Soviet Union with whom they sympathised and saw as the most implacable opponents of fascism. In the Thirties, this view extended far beyond the ranks of the CP.

By the mid-1930s, sensitive to the experiences and conditions surrounding the rise of Hitler in Germany, the NUWM increasingly found it necessary to oppose the activities of the British Union of Fascists (BUF).

The Leader of the British Union, Sir Oswald Mosley, had been a leading member of the Labour Party. In 1930 he resigned from the Party after the Llandudno Conference of that year rejected his Memorandum that largely dealt, as we have seen, with unemployment. He then formed the British Union, likening many of its policies to those proposed, but never implemented by Hitler and Mussolini. Like his mentors and funders, Mosley promised to abolish all unearned income, to confiscate all war wealth, to nationalise the trusts, municipalise large shops, raise wages, shorten hours and provide jobs for the unemployed. A sizeable proportion of his membership was drawn from amongst the unemployed. In many ways, in the public consciousness, Mosley was a one-issue man - unemployment.

In April 1936, a leading article appeared in the 'Fascist Quarterly' stating *"After the crisis year of 1939, the next depression will begin. How deep that* depression will be it is difficult to say...*As the slumps of the 1940s develop and unemployment creeps up over the three million mark, the suffering of the masses will demand revolutionary action either of the Communist or Fascist order"*.

By 'Communist', the BUF included the NUWM that it considered "a communist stunt organisation" and a defender of Jewish refugees. Fascists had wrecked the NUWM headquarters as early as 1929.

The NUWM were not slow to take up the challenge. An NUWM pamphlet 'The Menace of Fascism', written in 1936, stated "It is no longer simply a question of having the unemployed organised for struggle around the issues of work schemes, benefit standards and administrative injustices. It is now a matter of prime importance to extend the organisation of the unemployed; to build up the National Unemployed Workers' Movement in order to keep the unemployed under working-class leadership and prevent them falling victims to the false ideology of fascism".

It was from 1934 onwards that the BUF intensified their work amongst the unemployed, attempting to counteract the influence of the NUWM, perceiving the issue of unemployment as fertile ground for the growth of the fascist movement. Part of their programme was to compel the Government to improve the conditions of the unemployed by forcing the setting up of a large programme of Public Work Schemes, promising full employment and control of the capitalists who were 'responsible for unemployment'. In 1928, in Germany, there had been some five million unemployed. The action of the Bruning Government in reducing the scales of unemployment benefit, had helped to provoke widespread rioting. This fact was seized upon by fascists posing as defenders of the unemployed, whereby they managed to gain much support and a foothold amongst workers.

In Britain, the NUWM was determined that such a division between the employed and the unemployed, and particularly the movement of the unemployed away from identifying with the general labour movement, would not be allowed to happen. An editorial in Labour Monthly in 1937 set out the challenge. "*If today that great movement (the British Labour Movement) through division in its own ranks fails to protect the workers, in the present critical period, it can lead to a lapse of faith, a loss of enthusiasm for the Labour cause, a mass desertion from the movement and a temporary wave of inertia which will be seized upon by our fascist enemies in an effort to crush the movement for all time*".

The threat of fascism brought a new dimension to the challenge to the NUWM stretching it beyond concern with the day-to-day problems facing the

LRD

MOSLEY FASCISM

1D.

THE MAN
HIS POLICY
& METHODS

AUGUST 1935

LABOUR RESEARCH DEPARTMENT
60 DOUGHTY STREET, LONDON, W.C. 1

workless. It created the potential for new and quite different alliances and took place at precisely the time when the NUWM's leadership had been given a new, and much more flexible course arising from policy changes in the CP. G D H Cole says in his book 'The People's Front', "*it was the need for unity against fascism as much as the need to fight the Unemployment Act and the means test which forced the NUWM to take steps towards securing general unity in the labour movement in Britain, at a 'lower price' than was generally asked for*".

It is certainly true in that whilst the NUWM collaborated with local Labour parties and other sections of the Labour movement on the hunger demonstrations and anti-fascist activities, after 1936, criticism of the leading figures of the Labour movement was toned down. Hannington wrote "*In these critical days of conflict between fascism and democracy, it is necessary to warn the whole working-class movement against the dangers which are arising in the field of unemployment and to endeavour to arouse all progressive forces to an appreciation of the importance of co-operation and action with the National Unemployed Workers' Movement as part of the struggle against fascism in Britain*".

According to the NUWM '*every unorganised locality is a fascist danger spot to the working-class movement*'. This belief gave impetus to their work. Failure to organise the unemployed was seen as a real danger to the general labour movement. Anti-fascist activities were stepped up. Several pamphlets were produced by the NUWM National Council to shoot down the propaganda that the fascists were using to influence the unemployed. These showed how unemployment in Germany had been 'eradicated', firstly by compelling hundreds of thousands into labour camps, after which they were deemed 'no longer unemployed'; secondly, all those who were not open supporters of the fascist regime were denied unemployment benefit and forced to enter the camps; thirdly, in violation of the Peace Treaty of 1919 conscription was re-introduced absorbing millions of able-bodied men and women into the armed forces. Unemployment was further 'reduced' through the introduction of widespread land work programmes, often forced, which separated families and stimulated internal migration. Finally, the operating of one of the largest armaments programmes the world had yet seen solved unemployment. Many of Hitler's capital works programmes, especially that of road transport, had a militaristic dimension. Many thousands of opponents and German nationals were simply driven out of the country.

In this way unemployment dropped from 5.5 million in 1932 to 407,000 in 1938. The number in employment for the same period grew from 12.4

million to 19.5 million. During the six years from 1933 to 1939 the average number of hours worked by a German worker increased by about 20 per cent. No worker could change or move job without permission of his employer, a form of serfdom not seen in England for half a century. Further, when the 'need' arose labour could be directed to move around. The absence of trade unions meant little on-the-job protection. Annual fatalities in industry doubled per thousand between 1932 and 1938.

Germany was actually experiencing a labour shortage whilst Britain entered a mini-recession in 1938. How did Hitler achieve this? By keeping wages at starvation levels and taxes raised to an all-time high. The Government took control of all social insurance, raising contributions and reducing benefits. In this way, the State could raise funds to finance rearmament. So the truth about fascism was not that rearmament led to a diminishing of unemployment so much as the diminishing of the unemployed led to a financing of rearmament.

The NUWM was all too aware of the inroads made by the BUF amongst pockets of the unemployed in East London, parts of Tyneside and Glasgow. The BUF in London was effectively a radical alliance between groups of unemployed workers, the petit bourgeois affected by the slump and a few aristocratic ne'er-do-wells. They operated a chain of soup kitchens and housed hundreds of the unemployed at their headquarters. The uniform, (obligatory before it became outlawed in 1936), was free. Offers of a clean shirt, a full stomach and antipathy towards 'foreigners' may well have persuaded some unemployed people to join the BUF, but a balanced historical assessment would reveal that very few succumbed. What is more, some of the few who did, later crossed over to the NUWM that saw all but the most hardened BUF member as a potential recruit. To their credit, nearly all the traffic seems to have been going the NUWM way.

One point of interest arises from the clash between the NUWM and the BUF. It is commonly assumed that the Public Order Act of 1936, introduced by the Home Secretary Sir John Simon, was intended to deal with the paramilitary organisation of the BUF and the clashes that accompanied its marches. This view gains credence because the Act was swiftly introduced in November, as a result of clashes in Cable Street and Royal Mint Street when Mosley's march on the East End was decisively blocked. But calls for the kinds of control introduced by the Act had been made for some years. Outlawing of uniforms was but a minor detail of an Act that gave unprecedented power over assembly and protest to the Home Secretary. On adoption of the Act, he would henceforth be allowed to ban marches of any kind, on a pre-emptive basis.

In truth, the Act was inspired by a series of draft proposals made in 1932 and 1934. In 1932, the Government had been concerned by the violence accompanying an NUWM-sponsored series of hunger marches and in 1934 by the violence of the notorious BUF rally at Olympia. When promoting the Act, Simon cited a number of reasons in its favour, one of which was a fear that fascist actions in East London was leading to a growth of communism and driving the local communities, especially the Jews, into the arms of the communists.

It is naïve to expect the State to stand by whilst violence accompanies public protest. The apparent legislative attempt to tackle the BUF was really a subtle way of exercising greater control over public demonstrations. In the 1930s the greatest, that is, largest and most influential public manifestations were those of the unemployed led by the NUWM. Clipping the wings of the BUF was an excuse to also control protest against unemployment.

In 1936 the NUWM contingents took part in anti-fascist battles in London, Leeds, Glasgow and on Tyneside and numerous examples exist of their activity in this area. In issue No.1, July 1933 of 'Vigilant', organ of the Blantyre branch of the NUWM, an article 'Fight the danger of Fascism' speaks of the branch's progress in combating the Scottish Fascist Party that was stepping up its activities in the area. It says *"The idea is to get the Protestant workers in Scotland to regard the Catholic worker as the cause of poverty and bad conditions"*. Further, "No worker should allow himself, under any circumstances, to be deluded by the propaganda of the fascists; should absolutely refuse to break the ranks but fight all the time against this real and growing menace".

Table 27 Unemployment in large towns, July 1936

(Numbers of unemployed in thousands)

Halifax	2.3	Middlesbrough	10.6	Dundee	15.5
Barrow	2.8	South Shields	11.2	Oldham	15.4
Brighton	3.2	Salford	11.6	Sunderland	18.1
Huddersfield	4.2	Wigan	11.9	Leeds	20.1
Coventry	5.1	Barnsley	12.9	Edinburgh	20.4
Portsmouth	5.2	Swansea	13.2	Newcastle	20.6
Grimsby	5.6	Blackburn	13.4	Birmingham	21.7
Wolverhampton	5.9	Bradford	13.7	Stoke-on-Trent	21.8
Norwich	6.2	Hull	13.9	Sheffield	24.7
Plymouth	7.2	Nottingham	14.0	Manchester	38.1
Leicester	9.9	Cardiff	14.9	Liverpool	84.0
Doncaster	10.1	Bristol	15.1	Glasgow	89.6
Bolton	10.2				

Source: GDH Cole and MI Cole The Condition of Britain (LBC Gollanz 1937)

Many of the anti-fascist campaigns that the NUWM participated in were centrally directed, forming part of a national policy linking unemployment which remained doggedly high in many major cities, fascism and war, see Table 27. But it is clear that opposition to fascism was a popular issue locally and the fascists were monitored on a daily basis using local initiative. Circular E30 from NUWM headquarters calls for support for seven members who were sentenced to between two and 12 months hard labour in the Rhondda Valley, where they had been 'amongst thousands of workers who, despite police opposition, demonstrated and eventually broke up a meeting of fascists outside the Rhondda Labour Exchange'. Such action could never be directed from a centre.

Dated 13th August 1936, Circular E18 pointed to the 'grave situation in Spain' and called for meetings to be arranged in local cities to aid that country. "National Headquarters calls upon all branches and districts of our movement to associate themselves with other working-class organisations in solidarity activity with the Spanish workers. We should connect up the fight of the British unemployed against the new UAB regulations with the campaign of solidarity with the Spanish workers and in every way assist in building working-class unity against the Baldwin Government and against fascism... At all meetings

RESOLUTION ON WAR DANGER

(See supplementary material)

The N.U.W.M. has always declared its firm determination to support the preservation of Peace and in so doing has consistently opposed the policy of armament expenditure at the expense of the unemployed. Today we find ourselves faced with the most acute war danger since 1914.

This meeting of the National Administrative Council of the N.U.W.M., therefore, calls upon the working class to take all possible action against the robber war of Mussolini against Abyssinia, which if allowed to take place will encourage the other Imperialist countries bent on an early war, namely Hitler Germany, and Japan and Poland. Thus the war in Abyssinia will develop into a world war unless decisively checked.

The National Administrative Council calls upon all unemployed workers to participate in the struggle for the maintenance of peace, to support all forms of industrial action designed to hold up supplies for Italy.

It also calls upon the unemployed to support all organisations fighting for Peace, and the use of any and every form of mass pressure on the National Government, with the object of forcing it to cease bargaining with Italy over the question of the division of Abyssinia and to support those Governments, which, like the Soviet Government and the smaller states of Europe are standing for the complete independence of Abyssinia and the application of sanctions against Italy for the preservation of Peace.

Peace and War is in the balance and the workers must bring all possible pressure on the National Government to cease haggling and in concert with other members of the League to impose an embargo on all arms, raw materials and manufactured goods coming to and from Italy, and also to close the Suez Canal.

At the same time the National Administrative Council calls the attention of the workers to the fact that the aggressive attitude of Mussolini has been stimulated by the attempt of the National Government to drive an imperialist bargain with him. This Government can no more be relied upon to defend Peace than it can to improve the conditions of the unemployed.

It is therefore necessary that the campaigns for the defence of Peace and the defence of the unemployed should be directed to bringing down the National Government.

collections should be taken and forwarded to this office, from whence they will be sent to the fund which has been opened for the relief of the Spanish workers".

In his book 'Hermanos', published in 1978, William Herrick, a Canadian, spoke of the early months of the Spanish Civil War which he spent with the first British contingent the Tom Mann Centuria - later the Attlee Battalion of the International Brigades which was then being formed. Mann was honorary treasurer of the NUWM. Herrick tells of the nights of discussion around campfires where the main item was always the National Government policy of non-intervention and the conditions of the unemployed at 'home'. According to Fred Copeman, a one time leader of the NUWM who became a leader of the Attlee Battalion, *"of the first batch of lads, about 450 in all, at least 200 were unemployed miners from the South of Wales."* Many unemployed fought and died in Spain on the side of the Republican Government. Within fifteen months of Franco's uprising, three members of the NUWM National Advisory Council, who fought amongst the volunteers, had been killed: Bob Elliott, Wilf Jobling and Eric Whalley.

Such episodes, whilst often tragic, do serve to highlight the work of the NUWM against the onslaught of fascism. Of the reasons offered as to why the fascist movement failed to pose a threat in Britain, the most compelling is the united strength of the labour organisations within which the NUWM played its part. There is no adequate way to judge the success of the NUWM in combating fascism. What we do know is that Mosley's organisation never posed the threat that its fraternal movements did in Poland, Portugal, Spain, Germany and Italy.

By 1939, the question of war was not a new one to the NUWM. In 1928, they had led a campaign against what they considered was the threat of a war aimed at the Soviet Union. They joined others in conducting propaganda campaigns against the Japanese invasion of Manchuria and the Italian invasion of Abyssinia. In October 1935, the National Administrative Council adopted a resolution against war that read *"the three main danger spots from the standpoint of war come from fascist ITALY; fascist GERMANY; and semi-fascist JAPAN. In other words, fascism stands for WAR"*.

The NUWM campaigned around these points in the Peace Ballot of 1935. On sanctions against Italy after the invasion of Abyssinia, the NUWM stated *"The question of whether we stand for peace is not the issue. Rather, the issue is how best to maintain the peace. The use of sanctions to restrain Italy is based upon the idea that if all nations in the League are united against Italy, she dare not go to war... A defeat for Mussolini means not merely a defeat of his aims* to seize the only independent state remaining in Africa, but means a defeat for fascism as a whole — Put words into practice and organise against the war threat. If the power of the League of Nations checks the war policy of Mussolini, this would be a warning also to Hitler and Japan. It would be a victory for the peace policy of the masses of workers throughout the world".

For over five years, the NUWM also campaigned against repression in Germany. One major campaign in this field was for the release of Ernst Thaelmann, General Secretary of the banned Communist Party. Circular D65, released in January 1935, stated *"Our movement will not stand on one side in the fight to secure the release of Thaelman and the many other prisoners in Germany. We must add our voice to those in opposition to Hitlerism and War"*.

As we have seen, a significant number of unemployed, who had been active in the NUWM, fought in Spain after the fascist uprising in July 1936. The NUWM carried out a consistent campaign in defence of the Spanish Republican Government, collecting money and sending them clothes and supplies.

In an internal document of 14th October 1935, entitled 'Explanation re-vote on War Resolution', the NUWM states *"The National Administrative Council recognise that on other questions of political importance there are many shades of opinion as to priorities in our campaigns... The NAC feel that in the face of the present war danger (referring to the Abyssinian crisis) our movement must express itself in the strongest terms on the question of the fight for peace"*.

In reality, the NUWM was hampered from effectively campaigning against war until early in 1939, because it lay outside the arena where war could be stopped; that is outside the munitions industries, the dockyards and the armed forces. It was possible to have an impact outside the immediate field of unemployment when it came to 'restricting' the growth of fascism but to 'down tools' in opposition to War, as had happened in the example of the Jolly George incident in 1919, was impossible when one was out of work. In expressing total opposition to War, the NUWM allied itself with those in the labour movement who, in 1939 as in 1914, were in a minority and too weak to prevent it.

The NUWM certainly had one concrete opportunity to oppose War. It came with the introduction of the Military Training Bill, which reached the statute books in July 1939. By the time this opportunity arose, the NUWM, in the words of Hannington *"had conducted its last campaign"*, which had been to secure higher rates of winter relief from the UABs in the last months of 1938 and the beginning of 1939.

In the space of only four years, Government spending on armaments had

Circular No.D.97.   6th January, 1935.

To all Branches, Women's Sections,
         and District Councils.

CAMPAIGN FOR THE RELEASE OF THAELMAN AND OTHER WORKING CLASS PRISONERS IN GERMANY

Our members will have noticed from Press reports the horrible crime recently committed by the Hitler regime, namely the execution of Rudolph Klaus, secretary of the German Red Aid organisation.

The whole world was horrified by this crime and over 60 of our M.P.s protested to the Hitler Government against this act. Following this came the letter of resignation of McDonald, the League of Nations Commissioner for the refugees from Germany, in which he alleged that over half-a-million people in Germany are being crushed for no other reason than their inability to prove that they are of so-called pure German origin, etc.

The German Red Aid and the Commission against the Hitler Terror have collected information which shows that: 4,870 anti-fascists have been assassinated; legal proceedings have been taken against 5,425 anti-fascists; 20,883 anti-fascists have been found guilty; sentences of imprisonment totalling 39,792 years have been imposed on anti-fascists; over 100,000 years detention in concentration camps in Germany have been imposed on anti-fascists; death sentences have been imposed on 110; 60 anti-fascists have been executed; 33 have had their sentences commuted to life sentences; and 17 await execution.

This is the murderous and brutal record of the Hitler regime. Every day brings the possibility nearer of the Hitler murder gang attempting to do the same to Thaelman, who was such a courageous and fine leader of the workers in Germany against capitalism. For over 3 years he, with many others, have lain in jail awaiting trial.

Our Movement cannot stand on one side in the fight to secure the release of Thaelman and the many other prisoners in Germany. We must add our strength to that of the other organisations in fighting for this.

At every meeting we organise resolutions demanding the release of Thaelman and all other working class prisoners must be put and sent to the German Embassy in London. Pay a friendly visit to the unemployed association in your area and get them to do likewise. Make a request to the local Trades Council and Labour Party to take up the issue. Wherever possible co-operate with all other working class bodies in sending a deputation to the nearest German Consulate on the issue.

Don't hesitate to ask school-teachers, doctors, nurses to add their protest against the infamous treatment of intellectuals, workers and others who are now prisoners in Germany because they either oppose Fascism, or don't bear the label of being pure German, etc.

                                          Issued by the
                                  NATIONAL HEADQUARTERS COMMITTEE.

risen from £186 million in 1936 to £630 million in 1939. This figure represented some 13 per cent of national income.

Ever since 1934, the NUWM, (with mixed success), had fought the introduction of the Unemployment Act and protested against the labour camps and militarisation of the unemployed, but with increased spending on arms and the growing fear of war, there was a demand for the unemployed to be conscripted and given military training. Unemployment was beginning to rise again by 1939. In October 1938, 1,814,000 were without jobs, by 16th January 1939, the figure was 2,039,026, showing an increase of 700,000 in 18 months.

The first months of 1939 saw a campaign aimed at the 'work-shy' in the national press, aimed primarily at breaking down opposition to the compulsory labour schemes that, in 1937, involved more than 25,000 unemployed. It sought to create a favourable atmosphere for the safe passage of the Military Training Bill then under debate. On 29th January 1938, a 'Times' newspaper editorial asked, *"Why, for example, should it be necessary to recoil from the system of labour service instituted in Germany merely because in that country it is immediately precedent in time and openly preparatory in character to compulsory service in the army?"*

A year later, fear of Hitler's advance had changed the situation so much that newspapers could say openly what the NUWM had been warning of for some time. An editorial in the Daily Express on 20th June stated the case clearly, *"There is one section of the community, in addition to the lads of 20, which should be conscripted for six months' service. The unemployed. All of them, up to the age of 35, should be called up for military training. This measure would be in their own interest. It would make new men of them, as well as making additional soldiers for the state. They would be healthier and happier if they marched on the parade grounds instead of walking the streets. And they would have the pride of serving their country"*.

The NUWM took up the issue of the Military Training Bill and the implementation of Section 40 of Part 2 of the 1934 Unemployment Act which was forcing thousands into labour camps, likening such policies not purely to those adopted in Nazi Germany but linking them also to the international policies of the Chamberlain government. In the strongest of terms in a pamphlet written in 1939 entitled 'Beware!! Slave Camps and Conscription', the NUWM wrote *"To understand the real meaning of the move to make attendance at these labour camps compulsory, it must be considered in its proper relationship to the foreign policy of this Government. The national Government*

Beware!!

SLAVE CAMPS AND CONSCRIPTION

By Wal Hannington

PRICE ONE PENNY

Published by the National Unemployed Workers' Movement,
144, Holborn Bars, London, E.C.1.

has dragged the name of Britain in the mud. It has deliberately betrayed democracy and peace; destroyed the League of Nations and collective security; encouraged fascist aggression on every occasion. Lord Halifax, the personal friend of Hitler, is now behind this drive for compulsory labour camps for the British unemployed".

The Military Training schemes aimed to take between 300,000 and 400,000 young men a year into camps. They comprised physical drill, manual work, and sport with an emphasis on tight discipline, simple rations and a nominal sum of pay to be regarded as pocket money. There were also lectures on the Empire, national service and government and the conscripts were encouraged to join the air force, navy or army on completion of their training.

By now the NUWM, despite its deep roots, and the new growth of unemployment, were simply too overwhelmed by the issue of war to be able to mobilise effectively. Some correspondence and documentation exists of the effective work of the NUWM legal departments in dealing with individual cases of hardship among those conscripted and their families. But no evidence exists to show any concerted or widespread opposition under direct NUWM leadership, when the Military Training Act of July 1939 was introduced.

The reasons for this can be found with the advent of war. The Act and unemployment were overtaken by the war and increasing numbers of the unemployed were either absorbed into industry or joined the armed forces. With them went the NUWM, which was suspended by decision of its National Administrative Council some weeks after war broke out in September 1939. There is some evidence that the NUWM may have fallen victim to the change of policy adopted in 1935 and 1936 at the Seventh Congress of the Communist International.

At this gathering, the communists had to take action against the encroaching danger of fascism, in order to protect democracy and prevent war. The communist answer in all countries was to seek a united front of mainly working-class and, where possible, bourgeois, parties, replacing their previous sectarian policies.

In Britain, this resulted in the CP closing down a number of its satellite organisations such as International Labour Defence and the League Against Imperialism. This was an attempt to obliterate organisations that had been associated with the 'third period' and could potentially bring the CP into conflict with Labour. In his 'Out of the Ghetto', Joe Jacobs writes of a meeting he attended with General Secretary Pollitt and others, in which the NUWM was referred to as a CP-controlled organisation whose prominence was to be diminished along with the ILD. This was so that the CP could concentrate its cadre in the unions, a recognition that many of its members were again finding employment and able to make positive action against fascism their prime concern.

There was not just disagreement but confusion too. In September 1938 at its fifteenth party congress in Birmingham, general secretary Pollitt felt *"compelled to record a decline in the activity of the Party against unemployment"*. In addition he points to an *"insufficient support for the NUWM. Largely because of a misunderstanding of party policy in relation to organising of the unemployed. We fight to defend the standards of the unemployed to secure increases in benefits and relief scales, to popularise works schemes, but this can only be done by effecting the closest unity of action between the Local Unemployed Association and the NUWM. This again can be made the medium for developing the complete unity of all existing unemployed organisations and their ultimate affiliation to the TUC."* The audience to whom he addressed his comments was very different from those he addressed in the early 1930s. For one, most were now in work. The composition of Party membership included a broader range of worker including academics, artists and white-collar workers. It was not so much that any of the other 'unemployed organisations' represented a threat to the leading role of the NUWM. Rather that, failure to form a single organisation of the unemployed was a barrier to approaching the TUC to heal the rift and secure affiliation. In pointing to the 'confusion over policy' he continued, *"this has given rise in some cases to the false interpretation that we do not take any active steps to build up the NUWM...therefore the Party will have to give serious consideration to the best method of both strengthening the NUWM and the local Unemployed Associations and of helping forward the movement for one united organisation."*

The basis for such confusion and policy flux appears to be corroborated by a number of internal CP documents. One records that, in March 1931, 47 per cent of members were unemployed. Yet, by 1939, the journal Party Organiser barely refers to unemployment at all. The bulk of CP members was now employed and could hardly be expected to provide a movement of the unemployed with staff. Another, equally valid reason for the organisation suspending its activities became evident in the period following the 1936 Hunger march. The NUWM always experienced a falling away of activities following a March as so much of the energy of the movement was devoted to each of them and represented a sizeable organisational feat. At least five factors called the continuation of the organisation into question following the march.

Firstly came the dropping-off of activity. Secondly, a fall in unemployment led to a return to work for some NUWM members. Thirdly, the organisation was a victim of its own success — the Government was too wary to launch a frontal attack for fear of further solidifying the forces aligned against it. Fourthly, was the CP's necessary change in standpoint — it decided to concentrate its members, who were now employed, into the unions, to build and empower them. Finally, actions such as the hunger march had opened up the possibility of broad unity within the labour movement. For the CP, this offered a new more positive role with greater potential to realise their aims for better conditions and more employment.

The 'suspension' of activity of the NUWM, therefore, looks less like the manipulation of a 'front' organisation (which it never was) and more like a mature evaluation of the altering needs and circumstances of the mid-thirties. If one were to conduct a comparative study of mass organisations opposed to fascism in the 1930s, the NUWM has much more in common with the mass, voluntary subscription, Left Book Club, than it did organisations such as the International Labour Defence or the League Against Imperialism. As the organisation declined, the NUWM adopted new, limited 'shock' tactics, similar to those of the suffragettes.

A Restoration

This book has attempted to place the NUWM in both the economic context of the inter-war period and that of the general labour movement. In particular it has sought to elucidate the unique character of the organisation and the conditions that gave rise to it. Only in this way can we look at the experience of the unemployed and the NUWM and ask what lessons such experience holds for us today. It is time to restore the organisation to its rightful place. Right in the centre of the history of unemployment in the inter-war years.

Would an organisation such as the NUWM automatically arise from a period of widespread unemployment? Obviously not. It certainly did not do so elsewhere abroad, either in the same way or to such an extent. There is some evidence that the NUWM arose after 1918, not as the precursor of a new way of combating unemployment, but rather as the last of a series of similar organisations that started in the Later Victorian period. This is only part of the story.

Many of those displaced from their jobs shortly after the Great War and who provided leadership for the NUWM had been active in the Shop Stewards' Movement where they had experienced a lack of national co-ordination of their activities. The formation of a national focus and centre for the unemployed movement so early on was both a sign of the influence of the shop stewards and proof that they had learned from their previous mistakes.

But these players were looking both further back and further forward than their immediate wartime experience. Each was born during the last twenty years of the nineteenth century when the consciousness of the generation that formed the foundations of today's labour movement was being fashioned. They came from working class families, in areas and industries where workers were already beginning to organise, casting away the seesaw effect of casual employment and seasonal unemployment that had apparently always existed. They were born to see a new, stronger working class organise itself into unions that would become a normal feature of industrial life - not the kind that had previously grown up overnight and disappeared almost as quickly. They were raised in a pre-war era where employment and unemployment were interchangeable hats worn by workers in different phases of trade cycles. They knew of the marches to Trafalgar Square when the West End feared 'King Mob' of the East End of London, the free speech struggles and the Right To Work movement so dynamic in both the last two decades of the nineteenth century and the first of the twentieth. They were born into a period when society was beginning to recognise that unemployment was a root cause of poverty and ill health. It was in 1883 that Mearn's wrote his influential 'Bitter Cry of Outcast London'. During the next quarter century, employment and unemployment and resulting poverty gradually emerged into public consciousness. From the 1920s onwards, these issues came to dominate politics, right up to 1945. Only the War had a similar impact. In this period, self-education and collective advance became a characteristic of a class-consciousness that led many of the most skilled workers, especially engineers, miners and dockworkers, towards socialism and its Parties - first the Social Democratic Federation –next the British Socialist Party, then the Communist Party. Others were drawn from the Independent Labour Party.

From its inception, the NUWM positioned itself, not as a charity-gathering organisation, but as one whose successes would be squeezed from the Government through mass activities by their unemployed members. Central to this would be their relationship to and joint activities with the trade unions and employed workers. It was not all politics and never could be because of the community background common to the unemployed. The NUWM had a healthy cultural and social side to it. Not least it provided both support and a mental focus to those with too much time on their hands. Whole sports programmes, including regional football leagues were established; many jumble sales, hikes, chess competitions and other such activities were organised. In 1934, Hannington estimates that over 5,000 children of unemployed workers were taken on trips to the seaside and for picnics organised by the NUWM. But at all times, the emphasis was on a combination of open political activity and individual representation. Even where the latter failed, the organisation would resort to direct action as it had done in opposing evictions arising from rent arrears.

The NUWM aimed to draw all the unemployed under the banner of the labour movement, on which would be inscribed 'Work or Full Maintenance'. Initially they thought that this would be achieved through the unity and common struggle of both employed and unemployed workers and for some years it looked as if this might be possible. No such 'unofficial' organisation, outside the ranks of organised labour, before or since, had enjoyed such influence at every level, although degrees of acceptability varied according to region and timing. The labour movement of the early 1920s was one of greater flux and reformation than historians have previously supposed. Organised labour had yet to find a place for the hundreds of thousands of its members made unemployed, but it had not yet agreed a core philosophy on which unions could be formally built. Syndicalism lingered, industrial unionism sat alongside the advocates of general unionism and craft exclusiveness. So, there was room for an organisation for the unemployed, (especially one so openly in favour of unions), to decide how its members should be organised and help them relate to organised labour. There is some evidence that this, often stormy, relationship, was not beyond the bounds of resolution. But in a world where the Russian revolution resulted in the division of labour movements into adherents of the Second and Third internationals, unity became less and less likely. Only in the 1930s would the threat of fascism and war again force rational rather than partisan thinking to prevail. By then though, unemployment had ceased to be the mass issue of the time. Those denouncing 'War and Hunger' replaced banners that once demanded 'Work or Full Maintenance'.

The NUWM filled another kind of vacuum in a movement still coming to grips with high volume constant unemployment. Which counter strategy and programme to adopt? Talk of Full Employment belonged to a future generation, but its origins lay in the debates it had in the inter-war period. The NUWM claimed that only ending the capitalist system could cure unemployment. Clearly not all the members or leaders believed this, but by raising the issue, the NUWM drew in many who saw in it a way of telling the world that they would not simply lie down and starve. It was a way of keeping their dignity. There could be no future talk of Full Employment as an aim in itself unless Britain had already resolved not to return to mass unemployment.

The vacuum that existed was one of policy. As an organisation it is clear that its influence in propelling, indeed crystallising, the issue of unemployment has been seriously underestimated. One need only imagine briefly the impact of such an organisation today to see that it has been hard-done-by at the hands of historians who should have known better. This has not been an attempt to rewrite history or (as some seem now to want to do), make the likes of Richard III appear cuddly! The achievements of the NUWM are clearly demonstrable. But they will only be acknowledged by a generation of historians who want to know what really happened rather than passively accept what they thought happened after tuning in to a history channel saturated with analysis based on the lowered standards of historical investigation associated with the Cold War.

Perhaps what makes these historians uncomfortable with the NUWM is that it was not an organisation formed for the unemployed, but by them.

The NUWM did more than force the issue at a time when few political bodies had coherent plans for dealing with unemployment. The government only thought that it was their responsibility because they were made to. They feared the unemployed as a social force but were increasingly compelled to act. The men that we regard today as having helped the unemployed in the 1920s and 1930s, Beveridge, Butler, Bevan, Bevin and Keynes were, in fact, relatively weak voices during this period and were not listened to by politicians until the eve of war. Even those who thought that the Government could, (through interventionist strategies), have an impact on the numbers of those unemployed, or improve the health of the industries of those employed, were largely unable to translate such thinking into action. In the mid-thirties 'planning' meant town planning, not nationalisation. Mosley and Strachey went down this road, but even they were not able to translate programmes into practice. This then was the vacuum into which the NUWM stepped.

So the NUWM became a player, arguing for policy and forming increasingly powerful alliances to ensure that the Government respected the unemployed, despite the fact that its avowed strategy was the revolutionary overthrow of capitalism.

The perspective of the NUWM was set out in its rules and objectives:

> *"To rouse the unemployed to constant agitation and struggle against the whole problem of unemployment and against the peaceful toleration of poverty and to educate the wide masses of the unemployed to a realisation that only the destruction of capitalism and the conquest of political and economic power by the workers can lead to the solution of unemployment".*

From the 'Aims and Objects' section (i) of the NUWM Rules and Conditions 1931

While it never reneged on this resolution, it never came close to implementing it either. Some, including many well beyond the ranks of the NUWM, thought that revolution was a lot closer with the 1929 collapse. Instead, the NUWM began as a force criticising lack of strategy in all parties and the Government in particular for failing to deal with unemployment. It progressed to becoming a first class force of pragmatism, propaganda and representation. Above all, it got results – even from the very beginning. As early as 1921, it was able to sustain pressure on the Government, forcing a meeting with the Minister for Health, which was to secure agreement to pay for the dependents of the unemployed for the first time. Whereas, pre-1914 unemployment was dealt with largely through the workhouse system, by the late 1920s, as a result of the scale of unemployment and the activity of the unemployed, out-relief and mass insurance schemes had become the norm. Increasingly, from the mid 1930s onwards, as its adherents were drawn back into employment, it became a force for policy formation. It saw the opportunity to have influence far beyond its immediate ranks and took it.

At the turn of the 1930s the Poor Law was dead on its feet but a new system had not yet been formed. The NUWM seized the opportunity to wrong-foot this old foe before a new one could be brought into play. Often showing remarkable tactical ability (gained by some of its leaders from the trenches of France and Belgium), they were able to turn the locally accountable nature of unemployment relief to their advantage. The effects of this local tactical flexibility were all the greater because, in addition to the changing nature of unemployment provision, local government was, itself, undergoing radical change. In doing so, it influenced thinking about unemployment for generations to come.

This book has concentrated on unemployment, employment policy and the impact of the NUWM in changing public perception and policy. The impact, worthy of further study elsewhere, went way beyond this area, affecting culture too. In his book 'These Poor Hands', B L Coombes and many other worker-authors like him produced a kind of realism that contributed to a transformation of British literature and cinema in the 1960s. Organisations such as the Artists International Association, grouped together the cream of Britain's inter-war years sculptors, painters, graphic artists and photographers. In all of their work and many exhibitions, unemployment and war were dominant themes.

Nearly all of the union leaders, Labour Party members and MPs and a good number of Liberals, Commonwealth Party and Independents, who formulated the policies of Total War, the 1945 victory, nationalisation, formation of the health service and education systems, were influenced by key players who had either been unemployed or had worked with or been members of the NUWM. Read the biographies of characters as diverse as Manny Shinwell, Konni

Zilliacus, Harry MacShane, Harold MacMillan or Jack Jones, to see how pervasive and powerful the issue of unemployment was.

When Shinwell, who defeated Ramsay MacDonald in 1935, as cabinet minister responsible for energy, was able to sit down to draw up policies for the nationalisation of coal and the construction of an energy industry in the late 1940s, he drew on direct personal experience of the Hungry Thirties, unemployment and unemployed agitation. It is a touch ironic that the NUWM, long ostracised by Labour officialdom, did so much to change public perceptions of unemployment and, thereby, contributed generously to the groundswell of opinion that brought Labour to power in 1945. The generation of politician and trade unionist, schooled in the NUWM and coming to maturity in the 1950s, was a very different one from that which had drifted into the General Strike and the wilderness of the 1930s. The 1950s generation has long been underestimated and undervalued. Organisations such as the NUWM had shown that things could be aimed for, could be achieved and, above all, then be put into practice. The 1950s labour movement had passed well beyond the politics of protest. Jack Dash, official and unofficial dockworkers' leader in the TGWU and a household name, became a union activist and CP member after attending an NUWM street meeting in Stepney in London's East End. Clem Atlee, who as a Mayor, took part in most of the principal unemployment protests between 1921 and 1936 went on to became Prime Minister.

One of the great achievements of the NUWM is placing the unemployment issue in the political arena so that it could not be ignored. It helped to force those who for so long blamed the unemployed, (including the unemployed themselves, who thought their predicament was of their own making), to think again. The Government, was compelled to take responsibility for unemployment and the handling of the unemployed at long last. By the time the militants of the NUWM were returning to employment the organisation had stigmatised both the means test and the household means test, thereby ameliorating the basis on which the post 1945 welfare state was to be built. So hated and stigmatised was means testing, that it was only possible to reintroduce it in welfare benefits, after the generation that defeated the National Government, began to die out.

The generation of MPs who sang the Red Flag when parliament gathered in the wake of the 1945 election were all touched in some way by unemployment. But so were many in the Liberal party, in Commonwealth, in the Lords. A significant section of conservatism was also affected and influenced. Beveridge completely reconstructed social insurance through his 1942 report. For him the struggle was to eradicate Want, Disease, Ignorance, Squalor and Idleness. Ending unemployment was to be the way to secure these aims. He also said, in a declaration of principles, that *"a revolutionary moment in the world's history is a time for revolutions, not for patching"*. The plan to eradicate Want is based on a diagnosis of that Want. It is based on social surveys carried out between the wars. In part because his Plan reflected the experience of the inter-war years one of its first measures was to make benefits universal and do away with the Means test. The change was to be both fundamental and decisive and not "*to be restricted by sectional interests*".

In emphasising the importance of unity, it has been vital to try to reflect the significance attached to the issue by the organisation itself. This was not unity for its own sake, but because the nature of the British labour movement, with its single centre and discipline, provided no other option. Indeed for a number of years, the NUWM sought to argue itself out of existence, pressing unions to recruit the unemployed and retain members who were signed up, but who had lost their jobs. For all but four years (between 1928 and 1932) the issue of unity was the lynchpin for NUWM activities. There are those who would surely blame the trade union leadership for failing to achieve the desired unity. This is too simplistic. Where were the union members whilst their leaders looked away? For the most part, in the 1920s, they too were looking the other way. After the initial united actions in 1924 and 1925, which were successful, the souring of relations leading up to and after the General Strike, then a complete break, the NUWM were left in a semi-wilderness. During this period, their only real contact with the labour movement was as an affiliate of the National Minority Movement that was, itself, relatively weak and ostracised by most including the General Council of the TUC. If the NUWM was to shatter rather than change government policy, then the type of pressure which employed, organised workers could exert, was needed in unity with the unemployed. The ending of isolation and learning to work within the tradition of labour movement unity was what the NUWM had to face up to during this most difficult period for the unemployed, the inter-war years of the early 1930s.

During this time the NUWM had its greatest successes as an organisation. Time and again it achieved breakthroughs. In 1934, a month after the hunger marchers returned home, the Government raised unemployment benefits. In April of that year the Chancellor restored the ten per cent cuts in benefit to the level of 1931. It secured the rights to local individual representation at the same time as meeting government ministers face to face. The Lord Mayor of London

THREE DAYS THAT SHOOK EDINBURGH

STORY OF THE HISTORIC SCOTTISH HUNGER MARCH

By HARRY McSHANE

PRICE - - ONE PENNY

Dispatch Photo.
Hunger Marchers encamped in Princes Street—5.30 a.m.

Foreword by J. M'GOVERN, M.P. (I.L.P.) and AITKEN FERGUSON (Communist Party)

opened a £1 million fund in direct response to the impact made by the presence of hunger marchers in the capital. The South Wales miners' march ensured that those taken off benefit for taking part in strikes or being locked out were reinstated. Later, in Wales, the government established training centres. In 1928 in Scotland the NUWM organised a march on Edinburgh and secured an undertaking to root out unfairness in the qualification process for benefit from Ministry of Labour officials. It marched again on Edinburgh in June 1933 and had an even greater impact. A year later, the Minister for Labour suspended the thirty stamps clause for twelve months. This had been the central demand of the previous NUWM organised hunger march.

Mobilising numbers many times greater than its membership, the NUWM took on and actually halted the implementation of Part 2 of the 1934 Unemployment Act. Part 2 of the Act, as we have seen, required those receiving relief to attend residential instruction centres without wages. Dubbed 'slave camps' by the NUWM, they were smothered at birth. Unemployment was made the main issue of the 1929 Government and brought it plummeting down in 1931. The hunger marches were huge organisational challenges that dwarf any campaign conducted today. The 1934 march involved 1500 men, marchers from as far apart as Aberdeen and Devon; they passed through 188 main towns en route where they had to be accommodated and fed. They brought their own field kitchen and cobblers with them and even established a mobile barbershop. The achievements are there to be seen by those who want to see them.

Many of its best organisers: Copeman from the Eastern Counties; Kerrigan from West Scotland; and Will Lawther from Wales, went on to become leaders of the British battalion of the International Brigades during the Spanish Civil War. All were members of the National Advisory Council of the NUWM. They were prepared to pay the greatest sacrifice for the struggle against fascism and many more members of the NUWM went on to similar service. Their contribution and impact is more difficult to quantify but should certainly not go unrecorded.

The membership of the NUWM did fluctuate greatly. Unsurprisingly, it reached its peaks in the periods of greatest unemployment in 1929 and 1933, when Hannington in his book 'Unemployed Struggles' estimates a membership of 100,000. In his book 'The Inter-War Years', Ernie Trory, NUWM organiser in Brighton, claims that in the space of four months, from January 1934, membership of the Brighton branch rose from 120 to over 600 and within another four months *was again down to the 100 mark*'. It is doubtful that these fluctuations can be purely attributed to members gaining jobs and thus leaving the movement. Other factors have to be taken into account. Disillusionment which Nye Bevan called *"the greatest danger to the unemployed movement"* meant that many might join when activities, such as hunger marches, brought the movement to a high point only to leave as soon as the situation 'went off the boil'. Also, we have to account for the movement of workers from town to town. Others joined, much as they joined unions, to receive benefits or representation, only to leave when their individual problem was resolved.

The NUWM certainly drew its greatest strength in those areas where long-term unemployment was high, in South Wales, the North East and Scotland. The core of its membership were those long-term unemployed with varying degrees of political conviction, who stayed loyal while the thousands who joined, then left through disillusionment created the high turnover which led to financial instability and inconsistency in the campaigning potential of the organisation. Many look, and see, only this core of politically motivated members. But political motivation and even core memberships are not unusual in labour movements, or, for that matter, in most voluntary organisations. This analysis of only the core has led some people to see the NUWM as a CP satellite. They, therefore, miss the thousands of others who filled its ranks and misunderstand both the organisation and the lives of the unemployed.

By the early 1930s the NUWM had established itself as the pre-eminent unemployed organisation. It had seen off rivals such as Sylvia Pankhurst's Unemployed Workers' Organisation and the TUC-sponsored Unemployed Associations. Where non-TUC local associations were formed, the NUWM learned to live alongside them or simply swallowed them up. In transforming unemployed protest from charity mongering to aggressive attempts to shape government action, the NUWM became the organisation that others had to work with if they wanted to do anything about unemployment.

Continuous hunger marches from 1922, despite the boycott by the General Council of the TUC, gradually served to enlighten and galvanise large sections of the labour movement. By 1936, the hunger march against the means test was supported by Clem Attlee, Leader of the Labour Party and the London organisation was conducted by the London Trades Council, the largest in the Trade Union Movement and effectively the London arm of the TUC, which nationally was against the protest. It produced one of the largest demonstrations London had ever seen. What made this unity possible? Firstly, dislike of the means test went beyond simply those unemployed who faced it head on; for many it was government humiliation of the working-classes generally. Secondly, unemployment was very much a scar on the minds of many who had found jobs only as the economy picked up after 1935. Having been unemployed they never forgot the humiliation and poverty they had experienced and took these memories and the lessons they had learned with them into the trades unions. Thirdly, the growth of the anti-fascist struggle against Mosley and the solidarity shown in innumerable industrial disputes, proved that the employed and unemployed could work together and experience in these fields spilled over into that of unemployment. Finally, we cannot disregard the general attitude that existed within the working class at the time towards the domestic and foreign policies of the National Government.

What the NUWM did not do was develop policies for those organised in unions and in work, to prevent unemployment from happening. In this period class-conscious workers did not think this was their responsibility. Others thought that nothing less than the overthrow of capitalism, as in Russia, would work. In the many charters and petitions drawn up by the NUWM there were often references to reducing overtime, raising the school leaving age and a shorter working day.

Yet, nowhere was there much thought given to the investment needs, research and development requirements, trading paths, necessary skill and training measures for workers in different companies and industries. This aspect of class-consciousness developed later, first through Joint Production Committees in engineering and coal mining during the war and later still in the Seventies and Eighties when alternative economic strategies were being considered. This did not happen during the period under consideration because the NUWM were forced to the outside track and concentrated on the unemployed and the unions were weakened and on the defensive for much of the time. The TUC-sponsored Unemployed Associations were barred from discussing issues of employment and political parties and the Government, where they accepted responsibility, were slowly developing concepts of industrial strategy and interventionism. Only the Unions could come up with solutions and the author has sought to show why they did not. First and foremost the Unions were unable to see themselves as policy-determining players in an industrial arena and thus were unable to take responsibility for anything more than the immediate welfare of members. In concentrating on wages and conditions they missed the opportunity to influence patterns of employment, numbers employed and the development of the necessary skills.

By the 1940s this shortfall had been recognised. In coming to terms with a fuller role fostered as a result of the war, unions in Britain found a new level of maturity and an influence over society that was way beyond anything that could have been envisaged in the 1920s when the core aims and direction of the NUWM were being established. The labour movement that entered the Second World War was very different from that which later emerged in a number of important ways. In the process of shifting from a period of inter-war consolidation to a post war role of exercising actual power in politics and industry there had been a generation change. Those who led the movement in the inter-war years had been born in the Victorian era. Those who led it into the 1950s and beyond were born after the Great War and into a movement much stronger and more confident than the one that was established in the late 1800s.

In some ways, the later generation came to maturity in an already built environment whereas their forebears had to build the movement from scratch. As such the perspective and level of expectation of the two generations was quite different. The former had emerged from World War One and gone into World War Two scarred by unemployment and cognisant of the need to organise the unemployed. The latter emerged from the war having played a key part in the victory and certain that there would be no return to pre-war conditions, especially in the field of unemployment. That's how they voted in August 1945 and it was on this basis that they organised their own union-led intervention in industry. The motions to nationalise key industries were moved at union and TUC conferences before they were decided on and enacted by the government.

Given such success, why would the NUWM dissolve itself? The available answers are often too simplified but are understandable in the absence of detailed information. It is only possible to find one published reference to the break-up of the NUWM. Hannington, in his book, 'Never On Our Knees', written in 1940, speaks of a *"decision to disband the NUWM, taken by the National Administrative Committee (NAC) a few weeks after the start of the War"*. In the minutes of the NAC, filed in the Marx Memorial Library, there are no references to the meetings held to oversee the demise of the organisation. The 'Daily Worker', which regularly carried reports of NUWM activities right up until September 1939, carried no comment or word of explanation from Hannington, who was a regular contributor to the newspaper, nor from any other leader.

The reason given for the disbanding of the NUWM can only be partly understood, particularly when viewed in the light of the aims pursued by the organisation over two decades. It is said that the war effort, conscription and the growth of the munitions industries would put an end to unemployment and thus obviate the need for an unemployed organisation. Controversy certainly surrounds this view. If the NUWM had staked so much for so long on the claim that unemployment was a product of capitalism and could only be resolved by its destruction, what difference did war, (which the NUWM had been opposed to for years), make to this view? Had the First World War not been a period of high employment followed a period of high unemployment? The NUWM had no guarantee that this would not happen again, particularly after a war that many thought would be over quickly. Somewhere, evidence might exist that can set the record straight. A simple winding-down of the organisation might have been more appropriate but a winding-up is a different thing altogether.

The NUWM fell short of achieving its basic stated aims. The capitalist system was not and has not been destroyed despite being at the root of all the iniquities that the NUWM did so much to oppose. Unemployment continues its cyclical round of rise and fall. Its threat hovers over every worker today and will touch every generation of most British families. What the NUWM did achieve was the production of a generation whose political acumen ensured that every Government between 1945 and 1979 had to pledge itself to a goal of full employment. That, by any measure, is a tough act to follow.

Afterword

Having surveyed the employment landscape of the inter-war years, what can we learn? The NUWM proved that there is no mystery to organising the unemployed. Governments can be driven back. Acts can be changed or defeated. Political parties can be forced to confront the issue. Policy-makers can be made to do just that. Yet, as we have shown, to contest a rate of benefit may be crucial but it does not create a job. The challenge facing the unemployed is to find work. No self-respecting worker with the chance of a job with which to clothe his or her children would opt instead to remain unemployed. In that sense, an organisation of the unemployed, faced with such a choice – to work or not, will always have a limited shelf life. But an employed worker who understands the experience of unemployment is much better equipped for industrial survival. We should ask each one, *"Why wait until you experience the Long Weekend, before you start to consider what must be done to create jobs and make those we have, better?"* It is as if Rover and Fujitsu have brought us full circle. The Fujitsu experience has more in common with that of the pre-First World War generation. Rover draws on the positive experience of combating unemployment in the inter-war years. But it is a point of departure too. For the Rover workers who saved their industry and a whole swathe of the West Midlands, are employed. No Long Weekend for them. It is a lesson every employed worker should consider. Or shall we wait until it is too late and we are out the door before we ask the question? What work will there be? What kind of work can we expect? What future for our children?

BIBLIOGRAPHY

A Aldcroft – Inter-War Economy (1970)

Robin Page Arnot – The Miners, A History of the MFGB From 1910 Onwards (Allen and Unwin 1953)

Robin Page Arnot – The Miners, One Union One Industry (Allen and Unwin 1979)

C R Attlee – The Labour Party in Perspective (Left Book Club Edition 1937)

Tom Bell – British Communist Party, A History (Lawrence and Wishart 1937)

Tom Bell – Pioneering Days (Lawrence and Wishart 1941)

N Branson and M Heineman – Britain in the 1930s (Panther Publishers 1973)

A Bullock – The Life and Times of Ernest Bevin (Heinman Publishers 1960)

Keith Burgess – The Challenge of Labour, Shaping British Society 1850 – 1930 (Croom Helm 1980)

E Burns – British Unemployment Programmes;1920-1938 (1941)

FL Carsten – War Against War – British and German Radical Movements in the First World War (Batsford Academic 1982)

Hugh Clegg – A History of British Unions Since 1889 Volume III; 1934-1951 (OUP1994) Volume II; 1911-1933 (OUP1985)

Patricia Cockburn – The Years of the Week (MacDonald & Co. Publishers 1968)

Max Cohen – I Was One of the Unemployed (Gollancz 1945)

G D H Cole – Unemployment – New People's Library (Left Book Club 1937)

G D H Cole and R Postgate – The Common People; 1747-1938 (revised edition 1946)

G D H Cole – Great Britain in the Post-War World (Left Book Club Edition 1942)

G D H Cole – The People's Front (Left Book Club Edition 1937)

W T Colyer – An Outline History of Unemployment (NCLC Publishing Company 1934)

Communist International – Between the Fifth and Sixth World Congresses – 1924-1928 (London CPGB)

Arthur J Cook – The Non Politicals, the Spencer Union in the Coalfields (Labour Research Department 1928)

Frederick Copeman – Reason in Revolt (London 1940)

Richard Croucher – We Refuse to Starve in Silence: A History of the NUWM; 1920-1946 (Lawrence and Wishart 1987)

Mary Davis – Sylvia Pankhurst/A Life in Radical Politics (Pluto Press 1999)

Richard B. Day - The Crisis and the Crash, Soviet Studies of the West 1917-1939 (NLB 1981)

Georgi Dimitroff – The United Front, The Struggle Against Fascism and War (Lawrence and Wishart 1938)

Peter Dewey – War and Progress: Britain 1914-1945 (Longman 1997)

Ruth Dudley Edwards – Victor Gollancz, A Biography (Victor Gollancz publishers 1987)

Nina Fishman – The British Communist Party and the Trade Unions; 1933-45 (Scolar Press 1994)

William J Fishman – East End 1888 (Gerald Duckworth & Co 1988)

William J Fishman – East End Jewish Radicals 1875 – 1914 (Gerald Duckworth & Co 1975)

Hywel Francis & David Smith – The Fed : A History of the South Wales Miners in the Twentieth Century (Lawrence and Wishart 1980)

Hywel Francis – Miners Against Fascism : Wales and the Spanish Civil War (Lawrence and Wishart 1984)

Jim Fryth (Editor) – Labour's High Noon. The Government and the Economy 1945-51 (Lawrence and Wishart 1993)

B B Gilbert – British Social Policy; 1914-1939 (Batsford Publishers 1970)

S Glynn and J Oxborrow – Inter-War Britain : A Social and Economic History 1976

Arthur P. Grenfell – Afforestation and Unemployment (Fabian Tract 161 – January 1912)

JL and B Hammond – The Rise of Modern Industry (Methuen & Co. 1925)

W Hannington – Ten Leans Years (Gollancz Publishers 1940)

W Hannington – Unemployed Struggles; 1919-1936 (Left Book Club Special Edition 1936)

W Hannington – The Problem of the Distressed Areas (Left Club Edition 1937)

W Hannington – Never On Our Knees (Lawrence and Wishart 1967)

James Hinton – Shop Floor Citizens – Engineering Democracy in 1940s Britain (Edward Elgar Publishing Ltd 1994)

Eric Hobsbawm – Uncommon People (Weidenfeld and Nicholson 1998)

Eric Hobsbawm – Nations and Nationalism Since 1780 (Cambridge University Press 1970)

Eric Hobsbawm – Age of Extremes, The Short Twentieth Century 1914-1991 – (Michael Joseph Ltd 1994)

Eric Hobsbawm – The Age of Capital 1848-1875 – Weidenfeld and Nicholson 1975

A Hutt – Post War History of the British Working Class (Left Book Club 1937)

Tom Jackson – Solo Trumpet (Lawrence and Wishart 1953)

Julius Jacobs – London Trades Council, A history 1860 – 1950 (Lawrence and Wishart 1950)

James B Jeffreys – The Story of the Engineers 1800 – 1945 (Lawrence and Wishart 1945)

Katz, Podmore and Osmond – United for Progress, 125 years of the London Trades Council Movement (GLATC 1985)

Anne Kershen – Uniting the Tailors – Trade Unionism amongst the Tailors of London and Leeds 1870 – 1939 (Frank Cass & Co 1995)

C P Kindleberger – The World in Depression; 1929-1939 (Penguin 1987)

Peter Kingsford – The Hunger Marches in Britain (Lawrence and Wishart 1982)

J Kuczynski – Labour Conditions Under Industrial Capitalism Part 1 Britain;1750-1944 (Muller Publishers 1944)

Kushner and Valman (Editors) – Remembering Cable Street – Fascism and Anti Fascism in British Society (Vallentine Mitchell – 2000)

Richard Kisch – The Days of the Good Soldiers (Journeyman Press 1985)

Robert Lekachman – The Age of Keynes, A Biographical Study (Penguin 1966)

H.Lee and E. Archbold Social Democracy in Britain (SDF Press)

Jack London – The People of the Abyss (Pluto Press Classics-1993)

John Lovell – Stevedores and Dockers (Augustus M. Kelley Publishers 1969)

A Lozovsky – Marx and the Trade Unions (Lawrence and Wishart – 1935)

J.Ramsey MacDonald – Parliament and Revolution (National Labour Press 1919)

Harry Macshane – No Mean Fighter (Pluto Press Publishers 1977)

L J MacFarlane – The British Communist Party: Its Origin and Development until 1929 (MacGibbon and Kee 1966)

John Mahon– A Biography of Harry Pollitt (Lawrence and Wishart 1976)

Ivor Mairants – My Fifty Fretting year's (Ashley Mark Publishing Company – 1980)

William Mellor – Direct Action (Parsons 1920)

J E Mortimer – History of the Boilermakers' Society Volume 2 (1906-1939, London 1982)

C Loch-Mowatt – Britain Between the Wars; 1918-1940 (Methuen 1955)

Will Paynter – My Generation (Allen and Unwin 1932)

S Pollard – The Development of the British Economy; 1914-1967 (Arnold Publishers)

Profintern – Resolutions and Proceedings of the Fifth World Congress of the Red International of Labour Unions (Moscow /London – August 1930)

William Rust – Britons in Spain – A History of the British Battalion of the XVth International Brigade (Lawrence and Wishart 1939)

Jonathan Scheer – Ben Tillett – [biography] (Croom Helm Ltd 1982)

R Skidelsky – Politicians and the Slump (Macmillan 1967)

A.J.P.Taylor – English History 1914-1945 (Oxford University Press – 1967)

Will Thorne – My Life's Battles (Lawrence and Wishart 1985)

Nigel Todd – In Excited Times: the People Against the Blackshirts (Bewick Press 1995)

E Trory – Britain Between the Wars (Farleigh Publishers 1974)

Sidney Webb – The Story of the Durham Miners 1661 – 1921 (Joint Publishers Fabian Society and the Labour Publishing Company Ltd – 1921)

Sidney Webb and Beatrice Webb – Problems of Modern Industry (Longmans, Green & Co 1902)

Sidney Webb – The Roots of Labour Unrest (Fabian tract No 196)

Sidney Webb – The War and the Workers, Handbook of Some Immediate Measures to Prevent Unemployment and Relieve Distress (Fabian tract No 176 September 1914)

Ellen Wilkinson – Clash – George G Harrop – 1929

Williams, Williams and Thomas – Why are the British Bad at Manufacturing? (Routledge and Kegan Paul 1984)

J.M.Winter – Socialism and the Challenge of War, Ideas and Politics in Britain 1912-1918 (Routledge and Kegan Paul 1974)

BIBLIOGRAPHY; REPORTS; JOURNALS; PAMPHLETS

Reports and proceedings of the National Conference of the National Unemployed Workers' Movement for the years 1924, 1926, 1932, 1933, 1934 and 1936.

Report and Proceedings of 'Congress of Unity and Action' (1934)

Harry Pollitt – Political Reports to the 12th and 13th Congress of the Communist Party – Source: Selected Articles and Speeches, Volume 1 (Lawrence and Wishart 1953)

Harry Pollitt – Into Action! Written Report to the National Hunger March and Congress; February 1934

Magazines, Journals and Newspapers

The Daily Worker – selected articles:
years 1931, 1932, 1933, 1934, 1935, 1936, 1939 and 1940

Labour Monthly – selected articles:
1921-1924, 1929-1932, and 1934-1938

The Unemployed Leader – newspaper of the NUWM:
Various editions between 1932-1937

Society for the Study of Labour History
Bulletin No. 37 (1978), Bulletin No. 38 (1979)

'The Times' Newspaper – selected articles:
1st January 1931, 25th February 1931, 6th August 1931, 19th August 1931, 24th August 1931, 31st August 1931, 2nd September 1931, 12th September 1931, 29th October 1931 – Source: Times Report of the National Government 1931 (Published Times Books 1975)

The Labour Monthly – selected articles:
R Page -Arnot – The Labour Movement and the unemployed; 1924
Pat Devine – The Struggles of the Unemployed; 1929
F Douglas – Organising 'Slave Labour' in Britain; 1931
W M Gallacher -Advancing the Fight of the Unemployed; 1936
J Gollan -The Congress of Action and Youth in Industry;1934
W Hannington -The Problem of the Distressed Areas Part 1 and 2; 1937
W Hannington – The Meaning of the New Unemployment Bill; 1934
E Stanley – The Unemployed; 1924
E Woolley – Organising the Fight Against the Means Test; 1936

Pamphlets

T Bell – Why This Unemployment – (CPGB 1927)

The Record of the Labour Government – (CPGB 1925)

'50,000,000 Unemployed' – (CPGB 1933)

J Walton Newbold MP – Unemployment and How to Deal with It – (1924)

Young Communist League – Give Us Jobs – (1929)

J Winternitz – Problem of Full Employment

Lloyd George and Unemployment Insurance

Sir William Beveridge – Full Employment in a Free Society – (1944)

O Piatnitsky – Problem of Unemployed and the Tasks of Communists: A World Survey – (1933)

W Hannington – Our March Against the Starvation Government – (September 1928)

A J Cook & W Hannington – The March of the Miners – (1927)

J R Campbell – Only Communism can Conquer Unemployment – (1929)

W Hannington – The Problem of the Distressed Areas – (1937)

The Real Scandal of the Dole – (National Minority Movement Publication Ward undated)

Syd Elias – The Royal Commissions Final Attack – (1935)

Why We Are Marching

Programmes and routes of the hunger marches of: 1927, 1928, 1932, 1934, 1936

Joan Robinson – The Problem of Full Employment

Unemployment – A Labour Policy – (TUC 1921)

Who Prevents the United Front – (NUWM Publication 1927?)

The Unemployed Regulations Must Go – (London Trades Council 1936)

Ernie Bevin – My Plan for Two Million Workless

The Royal Commission on Unemployed Insurance

Walter Citrine – The TUC and State Provision of Unemployment Benefit – (1931)

Unemployed Women and the Slave Bill – (NUWM 1935)

Unemployed Bill and Women in Industry – (NUWM 1935)

J Ramsey MacDonald – New Unemployed Bill of the Labour Party

How to Fight the Means Test – pamphlet arising from the NUWM Conference against the Means Test (May 1932)

S Elias, T Mann, P Wall – Our Reply to the Royal Commission – (NUWM 1931)

'Unemployment' – Mosley's Commons Speech (May 1930)

Exposure of Belmont Slave Colony – (NUWM May 1938)

Our Case for the Unemployed Charter – (NUWM 1929?)

Sid Elias – Mass Murder – An Exposure of the Means Test – (undated)

The Insurgents in London – Story of the National Hunger March – (1923)

W Hannington (1932)

Fair Play for the Unemployed – TUC Case Against the Royal Commission (TUC 1931)

Unemployment and the Cost of Living – (TUC W Citrine undated)

W Hannington – 'Unemployed – Unite' – (NUWM undated)

W Hannington – Work for Wages not Slave Camps – (undated)

W Hannington – Beware of Slave Camps and Conscription – (1939)

W Hannington – Fascist Danger and the Unemployed – (1939)

W Hannington – 'Crimes Against the Unemployed' – (1932)

W Hannington – Chamberlain – Face the Fact – (May 1939)

W Hannington – A Short History of the NUWM (20 pages) – (1937)

W Hannington – 'Unemployed – Into Action!' – (undated)

'No More Depressed Areas' – (CPGB 1945)